Hidden Lon

The Individu

Jan Collie

PSP
The Pocket-Sized Press
Cambridge

PSP

The Pocket-Sized Press
Cambridge

First Published 1998.
Reprinted 2000, 2002, 2004
Second Edition 2006.

The Pocket-Sized Press,
2, Rosemary Lane,
Sutton,
Ely,
Cambridge.
CB6 2NZ

ISBN 0 9532491 1 5

Author's Note

Hidden London sprang from my own obsession with a city which is as full of secrets as it is of contradictions.

London seems to change from moment to moment, the shift from shadow to light sudden and striking, stripping off face after face without ever revealing all

London is elegant and ugly, manic and peaceful, mundane and magnificent – all things to all comers, in fact. It is left to the individual to interpret what they see.

And beyond each façade there is more. Always something more concealed in an unlikely corner, adding to the thrill of the chase.

Essentially a collection of quirky yet interesting facts, Hidden London aims to inspire anyone who enjoys off-beat information with an historical bent. There are currently five sections, each colour coded for easy reference and with their own contents listing. Cross references are picked out by colour and page number within each section.

I hope you will enjoy Hidden London and that it will whet your appetite for adventures of your own. I should point out that all the information to be found here has been personally researched and is accurate to the best of my belief.

Jan Collie

Cambridge 2006

Contents

Hidden London

Museums
&
Historic Houses

Contents

The Abbey Treasures

Westminster Abbey, SW1.

The most haunting and human portraits of some of Britain's best known Kings and Queens are not to be found in an art gallery, but behind an ancient oak door set into the wall of the East Cloister in Westminster Abbey.

There, in the Norman Undercroft, stand waxen images of Elizabeth I, Charles II , Queen Anne and William and Mary that are not only life-sized but true to life.

For these are no ordinary waxworks; they are effigies either modelled while the monarchs were still alive or very shortly after death. And as such, they represent the most faithful likeness to these people that it's possible to find.

But the physical resemblance does not stop there. It is made all the more powerful by the fact that the models still appear as they did originally, dressed in the type of clothes they were known to wear by the people who attended them every day.

This curious collection, now part of Westminster Abbey Museum, is what remains of what was once a large exhibition of funeral effigies. They were made for every monarch from the time of Henry V until around 1700 and were carried on top of their coffins as they made their last journey through the streets of London.

The figures, which were usually displayed in the Abbey as a memorial until the sovereign's tomb was complete, were kept by the minor cannons as a kind of side show. For a fee, the inquisitive could view the 'Ragged Regiment' or 'Play of Dead Folks', as it was known, and this provided the monks with a much-needed income. So popular was this entertainment that commemorative effigies of monarchs pre-dating Henry V were added to the collection.

Royalty were not the only ones to be represented here, though. Famous figures who could afford the conceit of a funeral effigy also had them made. One of the most interesting to survive the centuries is that of Frances, Duchess of Richmond. The Duchess, whose looks earned her the title 'La Belle Stuart', is believed to have posed as Britannia when Charles II decided to reintroduce the image on coins of the realm. Britannia is still the seal of the Bank of England and she appears on every one of its notes.

Until the death of Henry V, the practice at royal funerals had been to carry the embalmed body of the monarch through the streets of London to Westminster

Abbey with its face uncovered. It is not clear why representations were substituted at this time, but it may have been because Henry V died in France and was brought home in his coffin. The effigy of Henry, made of leather, coloured, crowned and robed, was the first of its kind and started a new tradition. Later funeral figures were made of wood and thereafter of wax.

Of the surviving pieces to be seen in Westminster Abbey Museum, those interested in historical detail may like to note the following.

- The figure of Charles II robed in red velvet with lace collars and ruffles. Until 1815, this effigy stood over his grave in Henry VII's Chapel and served as his monument. According to the diarist John Evelyn, the King was buried: *'without any manner of pomp and soon forgotten'.* Probably to avoid disputes over which religion he died in.
- The figure of Nelson, which was made as a counter-attraction to his tomb in the rival church of St Paul's. Apart from the coat, the clothes are his own.
- The effigy of Elizabeth I, which is a restoration made in 1760 of the original which had fallen to pieces a few years before. The original was carried from Whitehall at her funeral on April 28, 1603. It is amusing to think that only a year previously, at the age of 69, the wily old Queen had 'accidentally' let the Scottish ambassador see her dancing to prove that she was is excellent health!
- Mary II and William III. The figure of Mary stands almost six feet tall and it is known that she was much taller than her husband. The effigy was cast from her

face after death.

- Queen Anne, her long hair flowing down beneath her crown. The figure was carried on her coffin and it still the only sepulchral memorial of her. The unfortunate Queen's many children, who died in infancy, lie in a vault nearby.
- The Duchess of Richmond (*La Belle Stuart*) dressed in the robes she wore at Queen Anne's coronation and with her favourite parrot by her side. The stuffed bird is the only one consigned to fame in Westminster Abbey.
- Catherine, Duchess of Buckinghamshire and that of her son, Edmund Sheffield, Duke of Buckinghamshire, who died in Rome in 1735. Both used to stand by her grave in Henry VII's chapel.

The Westminster Abbey museum is normally open daily from 10.30 a.m - 4p.m but may occassionally be closed for State and special events.

The Chapter House and Pyx Chamber are also open to view and are well worth a visit.

Another star attraction is the College Garden, accessible through the cloisters via Dean's Yard. Open Tuesdays, Wednesdays and Thursdays from 10am -6pm April- September and 10am-4pm October - March.

Nearest tube: Westminster & St. James's Park (District & Circle Lines).

The Bank of England Museum

Bartholomew Lane, EC2

Every type of coinage, from decimal through to Roman gold bars, an be seen at the Bank of England Museum where a large and interesting exhibition traces the history of the world's best known bank.

Housed within the famous Threadneedle Street building, the museum offers a mass of detail on every aspect of the bank's dealings as well as informative displays which chronicle the changing face of British pounds, shillings and pence.

Visitors step from the entrance hall in Bartholomew Lane into an astonishing reconstruction of the 18th century banking hall designed by Sir John Soane [17] where life-like models of clerks of the period busy themselves behind the mahogany counters.

From there, they can wander around various rooms staring into showcases containing bank notes, engraving tools, printing equipment, weights and measures - in fact everything that has anything to do with money and money production.

Ancient ledgers and other bank documents containing the signatures of famous figures such as William Pitt the Elder, George Washington and Admiral Lord Nelson are also on view here, which will provide extra interest for history lovers.

The Bank of England Museum is open from Monday to Friday 10a.m. - 5p.m.
It is closed weekends and public and Bank Holidays.
Admission is free.
Nearest tube: Bank (Central line).

The Geffrye Museum

Kingsland Road, E2

Anyone interested in home interiors through the ages will delight in the Geffrye Museum, a small but enjoyable exhibition set in former almshouses in London's East End.

The museum, at the heart of what used to be the cabinet making district of the city, presents a series of period rooms from 1600 to the present day complete with mantelpieces, doorways, carvings and panelling. A great deal of care has been taken to add the sort of incidental detail which makes the rooms look lived in and every item on show is clearly listed on helpful guides.

The Geffrye Museum is named after Sir Robert

Geffrye, Lord Mayor of London and Master of the Ironmongers' Company, who founded the almshouses in 1715. A suitably grand statue of him, complete with long wig, still stands below the clock tower at the building's main entrance.

Extensive new gardens have been planted at the Geffrye. There is also a delightful herb garden.

- As well as the period rooms, the Museum is notable for its comprehensive reference library and furniture trade archive. Anyone with a personal or professional interest in furniture can apply to see these records.

The Geffrye Museum is open Tuesday - Saturday 10am - 5pm. Sundays and Bank Holiday Mondays,12 pm - 5pm. It is closed on Mondays, except Bank Holidays, and on Good Friday, Christmas Eve, Christmas Day, Boxing Day and New Year's Day.

Entrance is free, but donations are welcome as this is a charitable trust.

Those wishing to view the reference library and furniture trade archive should write to: The Geffrye Museum, Kingland Road, London E2 8EA.

Nearest tube: Bethnal Green (Central Line).

The Museum of St. Bartholomew's Hospital

Smithfield, EC1

This remarkably well set out exhibition traces the history of St Bartholomew's hospital from 1123 until the present day. Filled with interesting artefacts and medical instruments that have survived the centuries, it provides an extraordinary insight into the development of medical knowledge and skill as well as the treatment of the sick over the ages. It is also a fair tribute to a hospital that rates highly in the affections of Londoners for its long-standing tradition of compassionate care for the needy and disadvantaged.

St Bartholomew's Hospital - almost always nicknamed 'Bart's' - was founded by Raherus or Rahere, a favourite courtier of King Henry I. Apparently something of a wit, Rahere was said to have loved the high life until he fell ill with malarial fever while on a pilgrimage to Rome. Having vowed to build a hospital for the *'recreacion of poure men'* if he recovered, he then saw a vision of of St. Bartholomew who commanded him to build a priory church as well as a hospital, both to be named in his honour, on a site that he would indicate. The Saint went on to tell Rahere to give only his diligence to the project, promising that he would direct, build and end the work.

When the courtier returned to England, he quickly got a royal sanction to begin building at Smithfield, then a flat area of land used for tournaments. And from the start, just as the Saint had said, some miraculous power seemed to take a hand. A marvellous light was seen to shine on the roof of the church as it arose; the blind who visited it received their sight and cripples went away healed.

By this stage, Rahere had taken the cloth and himself became the first prior of St. Bartholomew the Great. When he died in 1144, he was buried in the church where his tomb, complete with an effigy added in 1405, can still be seen.

Given its position on the edge of wide open fields, the priory church and hospital of St. Bartholomew was the perfect location for large meetings. One of the most famous took place in 1381when Wat Tyler, the leader of the Peasants' Revolt, came to negotiate terms with the young King Richard II. Full of his previous successes, Tyler made the mistake of snatching at the King's bridle. At this, the Lord Mayor of London plunged a dagger into his throat. Although Tyler was carried away living, some of the King's knights dragged him out of St. Bartholomew's hospital and beheaded him.

Even at this early stage in its history, Bart's hospital

seemed destined to witness the fluctuating political fortunes of the city and sadly its boundary wall became the backdrop for many more killings. Plaques set into that wall recall only a few of the merciless executions carried out at Smithfield over the centuries, the victims dubbed martyrs or traitors, according to the philosophy of the day.

The hospital itself has narrowly escaped extinction for political reasons too. When Henry VIII dissolved the monasteries, it barely survived the closure of St. Bartholomew's priory church. The King finally agreed to re-found the hospital in 1546 and a statue commemorating this occupies the arch of the hospital's main gate (pictured page 9). More recently, health service cuts also left the fate of St. Bart's in the balance but a long and bitterly fought campaign has now secured its future.

Having weathered the trends for almost 900 years, St. Bart's continues to concentrate on medical care and its museum very much reflects that practical approach. And that is no bad thing as the history of the hospital is very much the history of the community it serves.

As well as throwing new light on this subject, the opening of St. Bart's museum has finally made another of the city's secrets public. Part way around the exhibition is a door which opens on to the hospital's official entrance hall and a glance around this reveals an unexpected extra. There, on the walls of a magnificent staircase are two stunning murals painted by the artist William Hogarth [27]. These rare examples of Hogarth's work are worth a visit in their own right but can only be seen at close quarters on Friday afternoons.

The story behind the murals is quite surprising. In

something of a self-serving exercise, the 18th century hospital governors decided to commission an entrance hall and Great Hall in order to impress visitors. The *pièce de résistance* was to be a spectacular staircase enhanced by two giant tableaux. According to the fashion of the day, the governors approached a Venetian artist to do the work. When Hogarth, who was already famous - though mainly for his scalding social satires - heard the news, he went to the governors and offered his services free. Happily, they accepted and Hogarth was able to prove for all time that English painters could create compositions in the classical style as well as any Italian. This not only helped to change the prevailing attitude, it also paved the way for a new School of English painting.

Hogarth's tableaux, one depicting the Good Samaritan and the other Christ healing the lame man at the pool of Bethesda, are every bit as impressive today as they were when they were first executed. The artist's exceptional skills as a caricaturist are particularly noticeable in the second mural and it is said that the onlookers at the poolside were modelled on patients at the hospital.

- An extensive archive of staff, patient and treatment records can be viewed by researchers or members of the public by prior request.

The Museum of St. Bartholomew's Hospital is open from Tuesday to Friday from 10 am - 4 pm except bank holidays. Admission is free.

Guided tours of the entrance hall and Great Hall of the hospital are conducted on Fridays at 2 pm. Meet at the King Henry VIII gate on Smithfield. Admission £4 or £3 concessions.

Groups and anyone wishing to see the hospital archives should contact

Tel: 0207-601-8152.

Nearest tube: Chancery Lane or St. Paul's (Central Line).

The Royal College of Music Museum

Prince Consort Road, SW7.

The Royal College of Music Museum houses what is probably London's most surprising and most difficult to see collection. Tucked into the basement of the college building in Prince Consort Road, the museum boasts a clavichord owned by Haydn, a spinet that probably belonged to Handel and trombones that belonged to Elgar and Holst. Yet many who would relish the opportunity to see these and many other marvellous exhibits miss the museum completely because there is virtually nothing to advertise its presence outside. On top of this, the museum is only open two afternoons in term time (though at least the literature says nothing about there having to be in 'R' in the month!). So it is even easier to miss.

Despite these anomalies, the Royal College of Music Museum is a must-see. Arranged on two levels, it comprises a fabulous range of instruments from around the world, all of which are clearly displayed either free standing or in groups inside glass cabinets.

Just about every type of instrument is represented here from harps to hurdy-gurdies, from flagelots to pocket fiddles, many with exquisite handwork. Among the ancient pieces to be seen is a fifteenth century clavicytherium, the oldest keyboard stringed instrument in existence. Another item of special interest is a guitar on which David Rizzio is believed to have played. Rizzio, who was secretary and advisor to Mary Queen of Scots, fell victim to a political conspiracy in 1566.

As well as maintaining this remarkable collection the Royal College of Music Museum now acts as a key resource for those interested in making music as it was originally played. At least two orchestras have taken advantage of records and drawings in the museum's archives to reproduce some of the period instruments to be seen here.

The most comprehensive collection of portraits of musicians in the country can also be found at the Royal College of Music in the Department of Portraits and Performance History. There are around 280 originals and 7,000 prints and photographs. The department also houses other valuable source materials such as the UK's largest archive of concert programmes and the Organ Club's collection of 20,000 photographs of organ cases.

The Royal College of Music, Prince Consort Road, SW7.

Museum open: Wednesdays and Thursdays in term time 2 p.m. - 4.30 p.m.

Entrance fee: Adults: £2 , children and senior citizens: £1.50.

Group tours can be arranged via the Curator.

Tel: 020 7591 4842.

Email: museum@rcm.ac.uk

The Royal College of Music's Department of Portraits and Performance History is open Monday to Friday from 10.00 a.m. to 5.30 p.m. except for 10 days over Easter & Christmas. Admission is free.

Nearest tube: South Kensington (Circle, District & Piccadilly lines)

The Soane Museum

13, Lincoln's Inn Fields,WC2

The Soane Museum is one of the most remarkable and densely-packed exhibitions of antiques and curios to be found anywhere in London.

Paintings, gems, bronzes, manuscripts and marbles litter the rooms, halls and stairways of this lovely 18th century town house, which is tucked away in a quiet square between High Holborn and Fleet Street.Once the home of Sir John Soane, who designed the Bank of England, 13, Lincoln's Inn Fields is a monument to one man's obsession with art and architecture. And what a marvellously eccentric collection it is!

From Canaletto's sparkling view of the Grand Canal at Venice through to the alabaster coffin of Pharaoh Seti I (father of Rameses the Great), nothing of beauty or antiquity escaped Sir John's notice. Every possible corner is crammed with 'finds' that he couldn't resist, snapped up in the sales rooms or imported from far off lands.

Of the thousands of items that Sir John acquired in this way between 1792 and 1837, some of the most notable are the first three folio editions of Shakespeare printed in 1623, Sir Christopher Wren's original drawings of Greenwich and Hampton Court and Sir Joshua Reynolds' two sketch books of drawings made in Rome. There is also a fine series of Hogarths [27] to be found here, four of which - a witty and cutting commentary entitled 'An Election' - were bought at the sale of the actor David Garrick's effects.

The Soane Museum is open from 10 a.m. to 5 p.m., Tuesday to Saturday not including Bank Holidays.Also on the first Tuesday evening of each month from 6pm - 9pm when parts of the museum are lit with candles. Entrance is free, although visitors are requested to make a donation.

Access to the Library, the collections of Drawings and Manuscripts, the Archives and the Model Room can be arranged through the Head Warder or by calling: 0207-405-2107.

Nearest tube: Holborn (Central & Piccadilly lines).

The Wallace Collection

Manchester Square, W1

As gifts to the nation go, one of the finest and most generous must be the Wallace Collection - an exhibition of objects d'art so magnificent that it ranks as a miniature Louvre.

Once the private reserve of the Marquesses of Hertford, the collection is kept in their London home, Hertford House in Manchester Square, just a stone's throw away from Oxford Street.

Masterpieces from the hands of Titian, Rubens, Reynolds, Van Dyke and Canaletto line rooms filled with fine furniture and porcelain, all kept as if they were still for the personal pleasure of one family. In fact, part of the charm of visiting the Wallace Collection is the homey atmosphere that Hertford House retains. It has a character and warmth that is often lacking in purpose-built galleries.

Though the Wallace Collection is known by connoisseurs as 'London's best kept secret' it actually contains such universally famous works of art as Frans Hals' *Laughing Cavalier* and Fragonard's *The Swing*. It also includes a display of arms and armour, particularly of oriental origin, to quietly rival anything on show elsewhere.

These, and innumerable other art treasures to be seen here, were gifted to the nation by Lady Wallace, widow of Sir Richard Wallace in 1897. Sir Richard was the son of the fourth Marquess of Hertford, who Thackerey immortalised as 'Lord Steyne in his *'Vanity Fair'*. The author also used Hertford House as his model for *'Gaunt House'*.

A range of new galleries, educational facilities and a restaurant have recently been made available to visitors. These are the result of a £10.6 million project to extend and enhance the exhibition in celebration of the Wallace's 100th anniversary.

A quiet and charming enclosed garden, featuring Parisian bronze urns and a fountain with a golden snake, can also be found here.

The Wallace Collection is open daily 10 am - 5 pm except December 24 - 26.

Entrance is free, although visitors are urged to make a donation as the upkeep of the collection is completely dependent upon public contribution.

Nearest tube: Bond Street (Central & Jubilee Lines).

The Foundling Museum

40, Brunswick Square, WC1.

The Foundling Museum tells the extaordinary tale of one man's mission to establish London's first home for abandoned children. It is a story which starts in harder times, when unwanted infants were readily left in the gutter to die. The sight, so commonplace on city streets in the 18th century that no-one gave it a thought, cut Thomas Coram to the quick. Perhaps because he was childless himself. Perhaps for some memory left on a foreign shore. Whatever spurred the old sea captain into action, it not only rocked society in his own day but positively benefited the lives of 27,000 youngsters over two centuries. His legacy still bears fruit to this day.

As a campaigner, Coram was a force to be reckoned with. He quickly won backers for his philanthropic adventure, up to and including King George II. When the

'Hospital for the Maintenance and Education of Exposed and Deserted Children' opened its doors in 1739, it was established by Royal Charter. Very soon, it boasted two reknowned figures, the composer George Frederic Handel and artist William Hogarth [27], amongst its governers. These two were great benefactors of the Hospital. Handel stipulated that annual performances of his famous *Messiah* should be given to raise donations and, at his death, generously bequeathed the score to the Hospital.

Hogarth, for his part, gave some of his works and encouraged other leading artists to do the same, so that a gallery - the first public art gallery in London - could be set up to attract wealthy visitors and possible patrons. That collaboration and the success of the resulting exhibitions lead to the inauguration of the Royal Acadamy of Arts in 1768.

The Foundling Museum pays enormous tribute to these founding fathers, Coram, Handel and Hogarth, oddly enough, none of whom were fathers in their own right. Thomas Coram, with his genial face, is remembered in a glorious Hogarth portrait, resplendent in a scarlet coat. Handel's many scores, manuscripts and items of memorabilia, lovingly collected by Gerald Coke and willed to the institute, are displayed in a special gallery. Important paintings from the hands of Hogarth, Reynolds, a 21-year-old Gainsborough, Wilson, Roubillac and the like are also to be seen, all housed in rooms restored to resemble those of the original Hospital, which was on a site adjacent to the present museum building.

But this is the happy side. More sobering is the tribute to the lives of the many children who passed through these portals. Though all who survived infancy were found work or apprenticeships and some even grew to be men of social stature, it is hard to walk through this exhibition without an outside lump in the throat. The collection of momentoes - little tags of marked metal, sometimes painted with figures or a name - which were the last items left by desperate mothers in the hope, one day, of being able to reclaim their babes, is a finisher. Few, in reality, must ever have had the money or opportunity, despite Hogarth's sentimental rendition of such a reunion scene.

- The Gerald Coke collection of materials relating to Handel and his contemporaries, including manuscripts, books and libretti is available to researchers Wednesday to Friday. For appointments Tel: 020-7841-3603 or Email: handel@foundlingmuseum.org.uk

---

The Foundling Museum is open Tuesday to Saturday 10am–6pm, Sunday 12–6pm. Also open Good Friday and Easter Monday 12-6pm

Admission: £5 Concessions £4 Children up to 16 years free.

Special rates for school parties and groups.

Nearest tube: Russell Square (Piccadilly line)

Dr Johnson's House

17, Gough Square, EC4

Except for a small plaque set into its exterior, the fact which speaks most strongly for the former fame of this fine Georgian town house is its survival.

For without its connection with one of Britain's best-known and best loved men of letters, 17, Gough Square, would almost certainly have disappeared without trace in the teens of the 20th century.

Set in what is now a quiet backwater of the city, Gough Square was once at the hub of literary London. And this was so not just because Dr Samuel Johnson (1709 -

1784) made it his home for eleven years. Writers of every description crowded into the maze of alleys and streets that wove around the Fleet Street area, because it was the centre of the publishing industry.

In common with his contemporaries, Johnson moved to this district to be near his printer. And while the house at Gough Square was only one of many that he occupied in London, it is perhaps the one which best deserved to remain as a memoir. Here it was, after all, that the author poured his considerable scholarship into the first comprehensive English Dictionary - the book which was to make his reputation if not his fortune.

The garret where Johnson and his six copyists toiled over this momentous work must rate as the high point of a visit to this house. It is easy to imagine Johnson, in full wig and enormous jacket, pondering over his definitions in this gallery-like room, perhaps occasionally glancing out of one of the many windows over the rooftops of London for inspiration.

But it would be unfair to ignore the influence of Johnson in the other rooms of the house, especially since they have been carefully restored and contain many items of interest including, of course, a third edition of his dictionary. A facsimile version is kept on the parlour table, giving visitors the chance to marvel at the 40,000 words and 114,000 quotations that Johnson managed to compile in just seven years.

A statue of Dr. Johnson's cat, Hodge, looking every inch the pet he fondly described as a 'very fine cat indeed', has recently been erected opposite his old home in Gough Square.

**17, Gough Square is open daily except Sunday, public holidays and Bank Holidays May to September 11 a.m. - 5.30 p.m. and October - April 11 a.m. - 5.00 p.m.
There is an admission charge.**

Nearest tube: Chancery Lane (Central line) or Blackfriars (District & Circle line).

Hogarth's House

Hogarth Lane, Great West Road, W4

Probably the cruellest satirist of his day, William Hogarth (1697-1764) used his formidable talents to pour contempt on 18th century society.

As one of the country's leading painters, Hogarth had status as well as skill. He made the most of both to campaign against corruption of every kind.

With his unique combination of horror and humour, Hogarth was a much-loved critic of public morality. No vice or affectation escaped his steely gaze, and these he mercilessly lampooned in a series of famous engravings now to be found at his former country home.

Hogarth's House, a beautiful relic of his era, is hidden away behind a high red-brick wall beside one of the busiest roads in West London. But the noise of the traffic melts away as you step through the large wooden gate which leads into a garden seemingly untouched by time.

The garden has a history of its own, for the mulberry tree that is its predominant feature is at least three hundred years old. It must be one of few to survive from a time when the trees were brought to England in a vain attempt to get silk worms to breed.

The house, with its lovely casement window, also remains much as Hogarth would have known it. Damaged by bombing during the war, it was carefully restored by the local council.

The interior of the house has been completely renovated in recent years and contains a well laid out and informative exhibition which documents the artist's life and work.

When William Hogarth died aged 67 in 1764 his life and achievements were summed up in the following eulogy, written by his close friend, the actor David Garrick. It is inscribed on the front of the artist's monumental tomb (pictured opposite), which can be seen in St. Nicholas' Church yard, Chiswick Mall, just a few minutes' walk from the house.

Farewell great Painter of Mankind
Who reach'd the noblest point of Art,
Whose pictur'd Morals charm the Mind
And through the Eye correct the Heart.
If Genius fire thee, Reader, stay,
If Nature touch thee, drop a Tear:
If neither move thee, turn away,
For Hogarth's honour'd dust lies here.

Open Tuesday to Friday 1pm - 5pm from April to October and 1pm - 4pm November to March. On Saturday and Sunday, it is open from 1pm - 6pm April to October and 1pm - 4pm November to March.

The house is closed Mondays, Good Friday, Christmas Day and Boxing Day. Also the whole month of January.

Entrance to Hogarth's House is free although donations towards its upkeep are welcome. Parking is available nearby at Chiswick House Grounds car park.

Nearest tube: Turnham Green (District Line) but it's a longish walk.

Hidden London

Shakespeare's London

Shakespeare's London

While London has changed beyond all recognition since Tudor times, a handful of sites remain to rekindle the memory. The city that Shakespeare knew is still there under the surface. Rare fragments have even survived intact.

The search for Shakespeare's London takes some detective work and a little imagination. The reward for the patient traveller is well worth the effort.

Contents

The Globe

Park Street, Southwark SE1.

If there's one name that is synonymous with Shakespeare, it is that of the Globe Theatre. And it's a fair link - the theatre helped to make the playwright's career and the playwright has helped the theatre to go down in history.

The image of the Globe - a little thatched turret of a theatre with tiered seating and a raised stage - has become an enduring symbol of the Elizabethan age. Its popularity, then as now, firmly centred around a man who observed life with a humour and insight that has never been equalled.

This remarkable partnership, Shakespeare and his famous wooden 'O', lasted a scant fourteen years yet the memory of it has been preserved for almost four hundred.

While a beautiful and faithful reconstruction of the Globe (pictured page 1) has now been built on the Bankside, all trace of the original disappeared for three and a half centuries, a small portion of it only resurfacing in 1997.

The Globe was one of a number of public theatres that suddenly sprang up in Southwark towards the end of the sixteenth century. Although bull and bear baiting rings had existed for some time, until then plays had always been staged on church steps or in inn yards.

Built on a site on the south side of modern-day Park Street, the Globe was assembled using timbers from London's very first playhouse, The Theatre. The Theatre had been opened by James Burbage, father of Shakespeare's friend and fellow actor Richard Burbage, in Shoreditch in 1576. When the lease on the land ran out in 1598, Richard and his brother Cuthbert simply dismantled the playhouse and took it over the river.

The Globe opened for business in 1599. Its sign was Hercules carrying the world on his shoulders and an apt latin quotation 'all the world's a stage' was carved over the front. Ever the Jackdaw, Shakespeare reworked this reference from Petronius into 'As You Like It', a kind of educated wink to the intellectuals in the audience.

The theatre seems to have drawn good audiences from the start. Shakespeare already had a reputation as a writer by this time, as did Burbage's acting troupe, the Chamberlain's Men. The combination was a great success and Shakespeare set about creating a string of new plays to expand their repertoire. From then on, the group spent every Summer season playing in the open at the Globe and every Winter under cover at their sister theatre, the Blackfriars. Amongst the plays they performed during that period were: *Richard II; Romeo and Juliet; King Lear; Othello; Henry*

VIII; Love's Labour's Lost; The Winter's Tale; The Taming of the Shrew and *Macbeth.*

With two thriving theatres to run and frequent invitations to Court to fulfil, the Chamberlain's Men went from strength to strength. They quickly won the patronage of the new king, James I, when Queen Elizabeth died in 1603 and were then allowed to rename themselves the King's Men.

The official stamp of royal approval would have enhanced the status of the company no end and the future of the Globe was assured. The theatre was held in such esteem, in fact, that when it burned down following an accident with a stage cannon during a performance of Henry VIII in 1613, the public and the monarch generously found the funds to rebuild it.

The Globe survived until 1642 when it was closed by the Puritans. It was demolished two years later. A succession of other buildings replaced the theatre over the next three centuries, the last being a brewery. When this closed, the site became a no man's land, shielded from the street by a high wall and a steel gate. There was nothing to betray its history except a grime-covered plaque placed by a long defunct 'Shakespeare Reading Society'.

This was how the American actor and director Sam Wanamaker found the site in Park Street when he made a point of searching it out in 1949. Wanamaker, who was in England filming 'Give Us This Day' (released in the US as 'Christ in Concrete'), was so shocked that he decided to launch a campaign to rebuild the Globe. The scheme took just over twenty years to come to fruition but plans to reconstruct the theatre on its original site were thwarted. He finally obtained permission to build close by on the Bankside where work began in 1987. The new

Shakespeare's Globe celebrated its highly acclaimed opening season in 1999.

The site of the Globe is partly covered by a Georgian listed building, Anchor Terrace. The remaining area, which has been designated an ancient monument, has been laid with cobble stones. A brick semi-circle shows limit of the monument and, within this, a differently coloured semi-circle pin points the exact location of the Globe. The plaque which inspired Sam Wanamaker has been reset in a special surround fronting the site.

The site of the Globe can be viewed at any time from the street. A number of informative hoardings have been erected explaining the history of the area.
The reconstructed Shakespeare's Globe can be found at New Globe Walk, Bankside, London SE1. The Globe complex includes an outstanding exhibition covering all aspects of the theatre's history. It is open daily from 10 am to 5 pm during the winter and from 9am to 12 noon during the Theatre Season.

Bear Gardens

Bear Gardens, Southwark, SE1.

A single red brick house set among warehouses and offices down this narrow side street marks the site of the last bear baiting ring on Bankside. An unimposing building screened by trees, it now sits in a quiet backwater. Three centuries ago, this place echoed to the shouts of traders and the shrieks of whores as rich and poor alike came to sample the pleasures of Southwark's notorious 'stewes'. Located just a few paces from both the Globe and the Rose Theatres, Bear Gardens was at the centre of the entertainment industry. Bear and bull baiting were major spectator sports and there were several purpose-built arenas in this area. They were all great crowd pullers and a source of stiff competition for the playmakers.

Bear and bull baiting were immensely popular in Tudor times and even monarchs were pleased to spend an afternoon watching the gristly set-piece fights. Both Henry VIII and Elizabeth I visited a baiting ring that stood just north of this site, the Queen apparently thinking it such an excellent amusement that she took the French and Spanish ambassadors along!

The bear garden that occupied this plot of land was built some time later, in 1662 and although this was after the Restoration, other bear and bull baiting rings managed to survive the Puritan backlash while all the theatres were closed down. This seems a rather surprising choice, considering the strict moral code of the day.

So bear baiting went on all through the reign of Charles II and from its site in Bear Gardens, the Davies amphitheatre, as it was known, did a roaring trade. The attraction continued to appeal to all levels of society and both the diarist Pepys and his contemporary Evelyn came here to watch shows.

The tide of public opinion must have been beginning to change around then, though, for while Pepys notes that he and his wife *'saw some good sport of the bull's tossing the dogs - one into the very boxes' on the evening of August 14, 1666, he adds: 'But it is a very rude and nasty pleasure.'*

The house on Bear Gardens is now an art gallery with a udio where resident and visiting artists can be seen at work.

PRINTSPACE welcomes visiors. Open 11a.m - 6pm, Tuesday- Sunday & Bank Holiday Mondays.
For details of exhibitions, see: www.print-space.com

The exterior of 1 - 2 Bear Gardens can be viewed from the street.

Nearest tube: Mansion House, Cannon Street (District and Circle lines) or London Bridge (Northern Line).

Southwark Cathedral

(St. Saviour's, Southwark)
Borough High Street, Southwark, SE1.

How many hundreds of people pass this beautiful church each day without even realising it's there, much less what lies inside? Placed as it is at one of the busiest junctions in London and given that all that can be seen from the road is the upper portion and spire, perhaps it is not so surprising that the ancient St. Saviour's, Southwark, is so often missed. But it is a pity because as well as possessing a marvellous atmosphere of serenity and calm, the Cathedral building houses the most interesting collection of tombs and epitaphs outside of Westminster Abbey.

Southwark Cathedral is by no means a dusky repository for the dead, though. Throughout it's long history it has played a vital role in the life of London's South Bank and it has a surprisingly rich heritage as a result.

Unlikely as it might seem today, Southwark Cathedral stood at the heart of one of the liveliest and most notorious districts of the city. When the Roman Army made camp on the Bankside innumerable brothels opened to cater for the needs of its soldiers. Some centuries later, when the area came under the control of the church, the whore houses were still flourishing. Business continued as normal and the profits became a substantial source of revenue for the Bishops of Winchester, whose lands included this part of London.

Although Henry VIII finally shut down the Bishop's brothels, others took their place and Southwark's reputation as a pleasure garden went on undiminished. Of course, sexual incontinence was not the only form of entertainment to be indulged in on the Bankside. Theatres, bear-baiting rings and cockpits were amongst the amusements and hundreds of taverns also plied a fine trade.

A sort of Soho and West End combined, Southwark positively seethed with activity. This was the Southwark to which Shakespeare came with the Globe Theatre and he probably lived close by, in the shadow of the cathedral.

St. Saviour's was undoubtedly familiar to Shakespeare and he must have worshiped there many times. This much is borne out by the fact that the playwright's brother, Edmund, was buried in the church after his premature death in 1607. Since he was an actor, Edmund's passing would not normally have attracted any attention. Yet someone evidently paid to have him sent off like a gentleman.

The register states: *'Edmond Shakespeare, player, buried in ye church, with a forenone knell of the great bell XXs.'*

Twenty shillings was a considerable sum of money in

Tudor times, nevertheless Edmund was buried in an unmarked grave. A commemorative stone was eventually placed in the paving of the choir.

William Shakespeare's connection with Southwark diminished after 1613 when he started to spend more time in Stratford. Three centuries later, a memorial to the great bard was included in the Cathedral. Reflecting the tastes of the Elizabethan era, it shows Shakespeare resting on his side, his head cupped in one hand. Behind the reclining figure is a carved frieze of the Bankside he knew, including the Globe and the Cathedral and above is a modern stained-glass window showing scenes from his plays.

While Shakespeare was still a familiar figure in the parish of St. Saviour's, another famous Englishman was just coming into the world. Born to parents who had also made the long trip from Stratford-Upon-Avon, John Harvard [1] was baptised in the then chapel of St. John the evangelist on November 29, 1607. The entry with his father's signature is in the Cathedral registry and a copy of it is on display.

Harvard, who as all Americans know, was responsible for the bequest which started Harvard University , was brought up in Southwark and was educated at St Saviour's Grammar School. He went on to study at Emmanuel College, Cambridge and was one of several graduates of that college who later escaped the religious intolerance of the day by emigrating to the New World..

The old chapel of St. John, which has been rededicated the Harvard Chapel, dates from the 12th century although it is heavily restored. The East Window, showing St John baptising Christ flanked by two angels, was a gift from Joseph H. Choate, the American ambassador in London from 1899 to 1905. It was damaged by wartime bombing and was restored, along with much of the fabric of the chapel, thanks to funding from Harvard alumni.

Perhaps because of these strong cultural links, Americans have chosen to commemorate two other famous citizens in Southwark Cathedral. A plaque to Oscar Hammerstein, the playwright and lyricist can be found in the Harvard Chapel and another, to the actor Sam Wanamaker (1919-1993) whose extraordinary vision and tenacity led to the reconstruction of the Globe Theatre [1] on the Bankside, can be found beside the memorial to Shakespeare

---

Southwark Cathedral is open daily from 8am - 6pm. Visitors are asked not to sightsee during services.
There is no admission charge to any part of the church but it is suggested that you make a small donation towards its upkeep.
Nearest tube: London Bridge (Northern line).

The George

77, Borough High Street, SE1.

One of the delights of setting out to explore London is in knowing that the city loves to tease. Like an old coquette, she adds spice tothe chase by concealing her treasures in the most unpromising places. Behind the noisy, grimy facade lie all sorts of gems and The George in Southwark easily ranks as an outstanding example.

No more than a few feet from the main road leading to London Bridge, The George is all too easy to miss. For unless it's a weekend, the pace on the pavement is set by office workers who are always in a rush. A turn of the head at the wrong moment and The George stays shielded in its dark courtyard, oblivious to the world beyond its doorstep.

While London has kept a number of its historic pubs and inns The George is unique amongst its peers. It is, in fact, the sole survivor from a number of galleried coaching inns that used to line this route. For centuries, Borough High Street played a crucial role in the life of the city. In one direction, it led to the main crossing point into the capital over the Thames, in the other, it led to Canterbury, the country's principle centre of pilgrimage. As a result, the Borough was a jostling mass of merchants, traders and travellers at every hour of the day and night and, naturally enough, hostelries quickly sprang up to meet their needs.

The Southwark inns had a reputation of their own, becoming so well known that the mere mention of their names conveyed a certain atmosphere and character. The Tabard, for instance, was Chaucer's choice for the starting point of his 'Canterbury Tales' and the White Hart was both Shakespeare's setting for Jack Cade's final plea to his deserting followers in Henry VI Part ii, and Dickens's setting when introducting Sam Weller in *Pickwick Papers* [23]. The George stood between these two and, like them, was very much part and parcel of a life that often involved arduous journeys in appalling conditions.

The history of The George can be traced back to 1542 although it is likely that an inn existed here for some time before. It is first mentioned as the St. George and the inn sign still sports a portrait of the saint in full battle dress.

Like the other Southwark inns, the George was built around three sides of a courtyard and in Summer its wide, double-tiered balconies became an excellent vantage point for the plays that would be acted out below. Surprisingly, there were no formal theatres before 1576 and taverns provided both an instant showcase and a ready audience for the many troupes of travelling actors. This type of presentation was obviously popular and effective, for when the first theatres were built they were modelled in the same style, the only change being to shape the seating around a semi-circle rather than a rectangle.

With its roots firmly in this tradition, The George can boast with some certainty that Shakespeare was a familiar character when he lived and worked in this area. The playwright not only had lodgings close by, near Southwark Cathedral, but quite probably came to watch performances of his own and other plays here on a regular basis.

The George that Shakespeare knew burnt down in 1676 but the house was immediately rebuilt to the original template. It remained unchanged until the turn of this century, when it was partly demolished for the Great Northern Railway Goods Office. While two of its splendid galleries were destroyed, the broad sweep of the third gives a fair impression of what the whole would have looked like and it takes little imagination to conjure a picture of the past from the shadows of the now quiet courtyard.

Still functioning as a pub and restaurant and even as a stage set for Shakespeare's plays, in Summer time, The George has been restored to its former glory by the National Trust. A remarkable building from the outside, it retains a number of interesting features on the inside too, notably the high pine settles which divide the tables in the smallest of the bars.

The George can be viewed from the outside at almost any time as the courtyard gate is normally left open. The pub and restaurant opening hours are regulated by the landlord. Nearest tube: London Bridge (Northern Line)

Middle Temple Hall

Fountain Court, Middle Temple Lane, EC4.

There can be few places as breathtaking as Middle Temple Hall. Simply standing in a room that has remained unchanged for four hundred years is fairly awe inspiring. But to see the splendour of its double hammer beam roof and to admire the fabulous craftmanship of its wooden screen at close quarters is an experience in itself.

This extraordinary treasure, a genuine glimpse of Elizabethan London, is the focal point of Middle Temple, one of the oldest Inns of Court. Designed to impress, it is essentially a common room for members of the Inn who both dine and entertain here.

Middle Temple Hall stands in a courtyard at the heart of an Inn which has preserved its antique elegance and charm. This timeless quality - so well described by Charles Dickens in *Barnaby Rudge* [3] - lends an atmosphere of calm that is very welcome in a busy city.

Housed inside a red brick facade faintly reminiscent of an old public school, Middle Temple Hall was constructed over a ten year period and finally completed in 1573. Although there is no record of the cost, the work must have been fabulously expensive as leading craftsmen were brought in to produce a showroom that could compete with anything in the palaces and stately homes of the day.

With rivalry running high in the legal profession, the different factions were eager to out-do each other by building bigger and more impressive buildings. Even from today's perspective Middle Temple Hall has the feel of the ultimate status symbol, so members of the Inn during Tudor times must have felt that their compulsory contributions towards it were well worth the outlay.

Then as now, social climbing was a serious sport for ambitious professionals and constructing a dining hall of this quality had at least as much to do with attracting patronage as it did with serving the needs of members. The strategy worked thanks to Edmund Plowden, the barrister who as Treasurer of Middle Temple acted both as principal and chief of works. Plowden's unflagging efforts and faultless reputation won influence at the highest levels and the Queen herself became both a benefactor and guest.

Well favoured by the sovereign, Middle Temple Hall soon developed into a kind of club house for the intellectual elite. In those days, men from outside the legal profession could join the Inn as social members and a host of famous names flocked to enjoy the debates, gaming and various revels on offer. With England's golden age of adventure then in full swing, the list of regulars included a number of seafaring heros, the most prominent of whom were Walter Raleigh, Francis Drake, Martin Frobisher and John Hawkins.

Festival times were a particular excuse for lavish entertainment and Christmas - which then extended from the feast of All Hallows on November 1st through to Candlemass on February 2nd - was given special treatment. Plays and masques were a popular part of the fun with troupes of actors being brought in for the occasion. It was during these celebrations in 1602 that London's leading band of players, the Chamberlain's Men, were invited to perform at the Middle Temple Hall. They gave the first recorded performance of Shakespeare's Twelfth Night and the playwright probably featured in the cast.

The audience seems to have enjoyed the play and one eye-witness, John Manningham, who was a member of the Temple, thought it worth recording in his diary. He wrote: *"Feb 2 at our feast (Candlemas) we had a play called Twelfth Night or What you will, much like the Comedy of Errors or Menechmi in Plautus... A good practise is it to make the steward beleeve his Lady widdowe was in Love with him by couterfayting a lettre, as from his Lady, in general termes, telling him what shee liked best in him and prescribing his gesture in smiling his apparraile etc. And then when he came to practise, making him beleeve they took him to be mad."*

This relic, like so many others that have been preserved here for generations, is one of the marvels of the Middle Temple. As if the magnificent Hall were not enough in itself, there are also the contents, any one of which would make an enviable museum piece. At the head of the Hall, for instance, is the Bench Table. A staggering twenty-nine feet long and made of continuous planks taken from a single oak, the table was put in place before the Chancellors' Window in the alcove to the left of it could be glazed. The wood for the table came from a tree felled in Windsor Great Park and it is believed to have been a gift from Queen Elizabeth I, whose portrait now graces the wall behind.

The Queen's picture, a Dutch piece painted in her lifetime, is one of a collection of six which have been assembled over the centuries. At the centre of these is a fine portrait of Charles I on horseback. From the studio of Van Dyck, a good portion of the work is apparently the master's own. On either side of this canvas hang high quality pictures of Charles II, Queen Anne, James II and William III.

To the left of this mini gallery, back in the alcove mentioned above, there are two more treasures. The first, a battered-looking rectangular table with legs that seem to have been added as an afterthought, has a very colourful history. This is the Cupboard, a table which used to be used as a lectern in the days when a junior lawyer's training consisted mainly of listening to lectures given by senior members of the Inn. Today, the Cupboard is an important prop in a junior lawyer's graduation ceremony. When a lawyer is 'called to the Bar', that is, qualifies to practice as a Barrister, he or she steps forward to this table in order to sign the Roll. The honour is made doubly significant because the oak that forms the table top was given to the Inn by Sir Francis Drake. It is, in fact, a hatch cover which started life on a ship called The Pelican, better known by its later name, The Golden Hind.

Standing in the alcove admiring this amazing heirloom, it is impossible to miss the Chancellor's Window, which is another historic rarity. At a distance, the window looks like a rather elaborate piece of stained glass. Close up, though, the various sections of the window come into their own, for each frame contains a different coat of arms. Mostly Elizabethan, these are the arms of former lord chancellors, judges and ordinary members of Middle Temple.

A point of interest in its own right, the window has become part of a new tradition over the last hundred years. Legend has it that author Robert Louis Stevenson may have found the inspiration for one of his most famous books in the names shown on two shields here. One, bearing three deer on a burnt orange background, is the device of a certain Josephus Jekyll. Close by is the blue and yellow shield of one Roburtus Hyde. Whether the story is true or false, *The Strange Case of Dr Jekyll and Mr Hyde* was published in 1886.

Still central to the daily routine of Middle Temple lawyers, this remarkable hall is one of London's great survivors - the Great Fire of 1666 miraculously left it unscathed after the wind changed course and wartime bombing destroyed only a fraction of the Eastern end. Accidents of fate aside, there is no doubt that its near-perfect preservation is due to the devotion of members of the Inn. This, plus the fact that the hall remains essentially private, has assured both its future and an irreplaceable part the nation's heritage.

**Middle Temple Hall is open Monday to Friday from 10am - 12pm & 3pm - 4pm.
Guided tours can be arranged for small groups by written request.
Apply to: The Treasury Office, Middle Temple Lane, London EC4Y 9AT.
Tel: 0207-427-4800.
Nearest Tube: Temple or Blackfriars (District Line).**

Gray's Inn Hall

South Square, Gray's Inn, WC1.

A neat little building tucked into a corner of a quiet square, Gray's Inn Hall shows no outward sign of its historical origins or interest. With nothing to indicate its importance, in fact, nothing to draw attention to it at all, the hall stands in cultivated isolation, shielded from the casual passer-by.

The disguise is, of course, intentional. While the hall is open by arrangement, it is normally kept private. Now, as for the past four centuries, the hall is reserved for the members of Gray's Inn, serving their every-day needs in everything from catering to carousal.

In common with its sisters at other Inns of Court, Gray's Inn Hall is central to an ancient legal institution.

Although its foundation year is uncertain, records prove that Gray's Inn existed before 1388. The land occupied by Gray's Inn had been owned by Sir Reginald De Grey, Chief Justice of Chester and Constable and Sheriff of Nottingham in the reign of Edward I (1239-1307) and it is likely that a society of lawyers settled here permanently during his lifetime.

As an emerging professional body, the lawyers of Gray's Inn must have had a meeting place although there is no evidence of a purpose-built hall before 1545. The building then on the present site was reconstructed between 1556 and 1560 and this survived until the last war when bombing destroyed all but the exterior walls as well as most of the buildings in the surrounding square.

All was not lost, despite the Blitz. By a stroke of fortune, the hall's exceptional wooden screen had just been dismantled for removal when the worst of the bombing hit. Unable to contain the resulting blaze, firemen braved falling timbers and molten lead showering down from the roof to drag the screen to safety. Almost all of the sections were rescued and when the hall was restored the screen, a beautifully carved 16th century piece thought to have come from a flagship in the Spanish Armada, was put back in place.

Another feature of the hall to survive the war was the majority of the stained glass. Set into windows that were removed in the early 1940's, the different panes bear the arms of former members of the Inn dating back to 1462. One of particular interest, in the centre of the North oriel window, shows the family crest of General Monck, Duke of Albermarle and the man who led King Charles II's army into London at the Restoration. The South oriel window was a gift from the American Bar Association when the hall was rebuilt.

With so much of its inherent character salvaged and the rest - notably the hammer beam roof - painstakingly re-crafted, Gray's Inn Hall has successfully retained an atmosphere of age. Substantially the same today as it ever was, the hall seems close to its past, when powerful and dangerous men would meet to discuss the affairs of state.

Names notable for influence and intrigue in Elizabethan times were Lord Burleigh, the Queen's First Minister and principal adviser, Lord Howard of Effingham, the Admiral who dispatched the Spanish Armada and Sir Francis Walshingham, the founder of the Queen's secret service. The third Earl of Southampton, Henry Wriothesley, was also a member of Gray's Inn and it was through his patronage that a certain up-and-coming actor/writer was able to flourish.

That writer was, of course, William Shakespeare and he was just gaining popularity in 1594 when his Comedy of Errors was played in Gray's Inn Hall. The chronicles of the Inn comment stuffily that: *'A company of base and common fellows..* ' gave their performance on December 28 as part of the Christmas revels. The playwright was very probably one of the cast.

Of all the nobles and statesmen of the Tudor era, the one who left a lasting mark on Gray's Inn was the master manipulator, Sir Francis Bacon. Bacon, who courted Queen Elizabeth I's favour but never won it, became Treasurer of Gray's Inn and a prime figure in its development. As well as being acclaimed for his philosophical and scientific works - in particular *The Advancement of Learning* (1605) and *Novum Organum* (1620) - Bacon was praised for planning and designing the Inn's famous gardens, better known as the Walks. Records taken in 1597 show it was: *'ordered that the summe of £7. 15s. 4d due to Mr Bacon, for planting of elm-trees in the walkes, be paid next term'.* In the next year more trees were ordered at the cost of £60. 6s. 8d. Bacon's formal layout was very much admired and by Charles II's reign the Walks had become a highly fashionable place to be seen. The diarist Samuel Pepys was a frequent visitor, relishing the opportunity to eye the ladies and catch up on court gossip.

Although Francis Bacon was discredited for accepting bribes after becoming Lord Chancellor under James I, his many achievements did not go unrecognised. A statue in his honour has been placed in the pretty square outside Gray's Inn Hall.

Gray's Inn Hall is open by appointment only. Applications should be made to: The Treasury, South Square, Gray's Inn, London WC1. Nearest tube: Chancery Lane (Central Line)

Blackfriars Playhouse
Playhouse Yard, EC4.

A modern street sign and a fragment of an ancient stone wall are the only lasting reminders of a building that once housed one of three London theatres where Shakespeare trod the boards. With no plaque and nothing unusual to draw the attention of passers by, the name Playhouse Yard is the only clue to the historical background of this area. Yet it is one of few remaining that can boast genuine links with England's greatest dramatist.

Seconds away from the frantically busy traffic intersection at Blackfrairs Bridge, Playhouse Yard seems almost deserted by comparison. An unremarkable street at first sight, it is worth exploring carefully. Within paces, it leads to an obscured churchyard and a little maze of alleys which would have been very familiar to Shakespeare when he lived and worked here at the end of the 16th century.

At that time, Playhouse Yard was part of a massive monastic complex which had been confiscated during the reformation. The monastery, which stretched from Shoe Lane off Fleet Street right down to the Thames at Puddle Dock, had belonged to the Dominicans who were known as the Black Friars because of their habit. The whole district retained this name and when the old refectory was turned into a theatre, it was naturally used to define its location.

Public playhouses were formally banned here but in 1577 an enterprising choirmaster managed to set up a private theatre in the refectory on the basis that his boy singers needed a place to practice. The theatre closed in 1584 but the building was bought twelve years later by one James Burbage, the son of a carpenter and travelling player, who intended to open the theatre to the public.

This plan came to nothing initially. Burbage died before the work was complete and the local residents anyway complained that a public playhouse would lower the tone of the neighbourhood. Burbage's son, Richard, converted the Blackfriars back into a private theatre in 1597 in order to placate them but by 1608 he was finally able to open it to the public and it was at this point that he went into partnership with Shakespeare and other actors in the company that they had formed.

The Blackfriars Theatre was big enough to hold between 600-700 people and Burbage's company, first called the Lord Chamberlain's Men and then the King's Men, would have performed many of the plays that Shakespeare had written for their use here and at their sister playhouse, the Globe [1] on Bankside. The works of other writers were also presented here, amongst them Ben Johnson's *Every Man in his Humour* in which Shakespeare himself was an actor in 1598.

Unlike Bankside, Blackfriars was a fashionable residential area and Shakespeare bought a house a short walk away from the theatre in Ireland Yard. The house, which he later willed to his daughter Susannah, would have overlooked both St. Ann's church yard and another of the old monastery buildings, the Provincial's Hall. St. Ann's is long gone but a section of the monastery wall can still be found in the part of its churchyard that remains in Ireland Yard [28].

St. Ann's churchyard is open all week during daylight hours.
Nearest tube: Blackfriars (District and Circle line)

Ireland Yard

Blackfriars, EC4

When the young Shakespeare took the road from Stratford upon Avon to London, his head must have been full of plans about how he would make his fortune and become a man of property. As well as astonishing literary skills, he obviously had a fair amount of business acumen, and he managed to buy houses in both cities before he retired.

Of the few London addresses that Shakespeare was certainly associated with, Ireland Yard is by far the best documented. Now nothing more than a side street, it was then a main entrance to the vast monastery of the Black

Friars. The monastery buildings had been seized and sold off during the dissolution but they were mostly left intact. The former gate house stayed in place and it was this that the playwright bought in 1613.

Shakespeare was already well established by this time. Having gone into partnership with Richard Burbage and others in their company of players, he had a stake in both the Globe and the Blackfriars theatres and took a cut of the profits. Although he is known to have lodged close to the Globe, probably near Southwark Cathedral, Shakespeare chose Blackfriars when it came to buying. Not only was the area considered select, it also seems to have been favoured by artists. Shakespeare's friend the poet and playwright Ben Jonson had a house here in about 1607 and the painter Van Dyck lived here between 1632-41.

The gate house on Ireland Yard was an ideal prospect for Shakespeare. It was a good investment and the Blackfriars Playhouse was only moments away. But the final decision to purchase may well have been forced by fate - 1613 was also the year that the Globe[1] burnt down so the company would have had to transfer lock, stock and barrel to Blackfriars in order to keep working.

No doubt swayed by a combination of these factors, Shakespeare went on to pay £140 for the gate house. While no physical description of it survives, a deed of Conveyance for the property states that it was: *'..now or late being in the tenure or occupancy of one William Ireland... abutting upon a street leading down to Puddle Wharf on the east part, right against the Kinges Majesties Wardrobe..'* The King's Wardrobe was a department of the royal household. It is still remembered in nearby Wardrobe Place and in the name of the church of St. Andrew-By-The-Wardrobe [31].

Although he had been a prolific writer, Shakespeare's

output seems to have slowed down shortly before he bought the Ireland Yard house. As well as being popular with the public, his plays were given special prominence in the royal court, so he probably didn't need to work so hard as he had before. It's likely that he was setting himself up for his old age and planning for the future, too. He made a point of keeping the gate house in his own title so that he could settle it on his elder daughter, Susannah, direct. Separate provisions were made for his wife, Anne.

Shakespeare died just three years after buying the property in Ireland Yard. The gate house passed to his daughter, as he intended, and she in turn passed it to her daughter, Elizabeth. Elizabeth, who was Shakespeare's last descendant, sold it on around 1667.

Ireland Yard is an ordinary street. The only relic of the monastery buildings that once stood here - a small section of the wall of the Provincial's Hall - is to be found in the part of St. Ann's church yard that is still preserved here.

St Andrew By-The-Wardrobe

Queen Victoria Street, EC4

The plain design of Wren's last city church attracts very little attention despite its simple grace. Thrown further into the shadows by a noisy and fast-moving road, St. Andrew-By-The Wardrobe is even easier to ignore. Like a well-bred lady fallen on hard times, the church waits with quiet dignity for someone to stop and pass the time of day.

With its rectangular body and unembellished tower, St. Andrew's presents a no-nonsense image to the outside world. Its warmth is all on the inside, where a wealth of woodwork carved in traditional style adds a wonderfully restful feel.

Burnt down in the Great Fire and bombed out in the Blitz, today's church of St. Andrew is a complete reconstruction nestling within Wren's walls. The details - including the 17th century emblems on the ceiling - have been reproduced with particular care, so that it is difficult to tell that the church was out of use until 1961.

The history of St. Andrew's dates back to the thirteenth century when it was associated with Baynard's Castle, a royal residence that has long since disappeared. When King Edward III moved his state robes and other effects from the Tower of London to a large building close by, St. Andrew's became better known for its connection with the Great Wardrobe. The name stayed to specify its location although the King's store room is now only remembered in Wardrobe Place.

One of St. Andrew's proudest boasts is its connection with Shakespeare. The playwright worked close by at the Blackfriars Playhouse [25] for at least 15 years and would have known the medieval church well. He eventually bought a house in Ireland Yard [28], which was also in St. Andrew's parish.

In tribute to its most distinguished resident, the modern St. Andrew's now features a memorial next to the window in the west gallery. Carved in oak and limewood, the memorial includes one of Shakespeare's contemporaries, the famous lutenist, singer and composer John Dowland (1562-1626) who was buried in the churchyard of St. Ann's, Blackfriars. St. Ann's was not rebuilt after the Great Fire and its parish was afterwards merged with St. Andrew's.

In a rather fanciful scene, Shakespeare and Dowland

are shown kneeling on a stage while cherubs hold back the final curtain. Between the pair at the bottom of the plaque is the following inscription:

> *'If music and sweet poetry agree,*
> *As they must needs, the sister and the brother...*
> *Dowland to thee is dear, whose heavenly touch*
> *Upon the lute doth ravish human sense...* '

Appropriate though these lines may be in Dowland's case, they have only a slim link with Shakespeare. Although they come from *The Passionate Pilgrim*, a collection of verse published in 1599 without Shakespeare's consent but with his name on the title page, this poem was in fact written by one Richard Barnfield.

As well as this recent addition, St. Andrew's has acquired several antique fitments over the past thirty years, most coming from other London churches destroyed in the last war. As a Wren church denuded of its original interior, it was lucky to get a replacement pulpit from the church of St. Matthew, Friday Street, which had been built in the same period. The font and cover also came from here.

Among other treasures are a figure of St Andrew, dated around 1600, which stands on the north side of the sanctuary and an unusual figure of St Ann who is shown holding the Virgin Mary who in turn holds the Christ child. This statue, which is probably north Italian, dates to around 1500.

St. Andrew-by-the-Wardrobe is open to visitors 8.30 am - 6 pm Monday to Friday. Services are held at 12.35pm Monday to Thursday, 8.30 am. Friday and 10 am. Sunday.
There is no entrance charge but donations are welcome.
Nearest tube: Blackfriars (District Line)

Hidden London

Dickens's London

Dickens's London

Dickens frequently used genuine London sites as a backdrop for scenes in his books. Many of these still exist in quiet corners of the city and can easily be visited.

If you have a favourite novel, you might like to discover some of these places by following the links by book title in the contents table overleaf. Locations that figured strongly in Dickens' personal life are given in a second listing. These provide references back to the novels, where appropriate.

Contents

Sites associated with Dickens's personal life

London links in Dickens's novels

The Inns of Court

The Inns of Court were familiar to Dickens from boyhood and there are numerous references to them in his novels.

On leaving school, Dickens was employed as a clerk by a solicitor who had an office in Gray's Inn and it is hardly surprising that he chose that location for the chambers of Mr Pickwick's junior counsel, Mr Phunky, in the case of Bardell v. Pickwick. The author started work on Pickwick Papers whilst he was renting rooms in Furnival's Inn, on nearby High Holborn. At that time he was working as a reporter on the *Morning Chronicle.*

While Gray's Inn still exists - albeit altered by bomb damage during the second World War - Furnival's Inn was pulled down in the late nineteenth century. It's site is commemorated, though, by a plaque set into the wall of the large block of red buildings erected there by the Prudential Assurance Company. There is also a bust of Charles Dickens in the courtyard.

Just across the road from the Prudential building is the former Barnard's Inn, a collection of buildings now owned by the Mercers' Company. The company has redeveloped the site, but in Dickens' day, it had fallen into disrepair. He describes it scathingly in Chapter 21 of *Great Expectations*, when he has Mr Pip arrive there as a callow country lad fresh up to the city from Rochester. Poor Pip had innocently: "*supposed the establishment to be an hotel kept by Mr Barnard, to which the Blue Boar in our town was a mere public house, whereas I now found Barnard to be a disembodied spirit or a fiction, and his inn the dingiest collection of shabby buildings ever squeezed together in a rank corner as a club for tom cats."*

Also close by is Staple Inn, hidden to view behind a neat row of black and white half-timbered houses which date from the sixteenth century. The arched stone gateway under the houses still leads to the 'little nook composed of two irregular quadrangles' as described by Dickens in Chapter 11 of *Edwin Drood*:

"It is one of those nooks the turning into which out of the clashing street, imparts to the relieved pedestrian the sensation of having put cotton in his ears, and velvet soles on his boots. It is one of those nooks where a few smoky sparrows twitter in smoky trees, as though they called to one another, 'Let us play at country,' and where a few feet of garden-mould and a few yards of gravel enable them to do that refreshing violence to their tiny understandings. Moreover, it is one of those nooks which are legal nooks; and it contains a little Hall, with a little lantern in its roof: to what obstructive purposes devoted, and at whose expense, this history knoweth not."

The 'little Hall' is still to be seen although it is not officially open to visitors.

Staple Inn features again in *Bleak House*, where it is given as a favourite walk for Mr Snagsby.

Of all the Inns of Court that Dickens mentions, probably the best preserved is Middle Temple [15]. Set back from the embankment on a wide expanse of green, Middle Temple somehow manages to retain all the gravitas of a great legal institution within the precincts of what feels like a little village. With its winding alleys intricately laced between cool squares, stepping in to Middle Temple really is like stepping back in time. All of which makes it the perfect backdrop for a novel and, of course, Dickens uses the setting several times.

A very apposite description of the Temple as Dickens found it more than a century ago and very much as it is still to be found today, is given in *Barnaby Rudge*.

Chapter 15.

"There are, still, worse places than the Temple, on a sultry day, for basking in the sun, or resting idly in the shade. There is yet a drowsiness in its courts, and a dreamy dullness in its trees and gardens; those who pace its lanes and squares may yet hear the echoes of their footsteps on the sounding stones, and read upon its gates, in passing from the tumult of the Strand or Fleet Street, 'Who enters here leaves noise behind.' There is still the plash of falling water in fair Fountain Court, and there are yet nooks and corners where dun-haunted students may look down from their dusty garrets, on a vagrant ray of sunlight patching the shade of the tall houses, and seldom troubled to reflect a passing stranger's form. There is yet, in the Temple, something of a clerkly monkish atmosphere, which public offices of law have not disturbed, and even legal firms have

failed to scare away. In summer time, its pumps suggest to thirsty idlers, springs cooler, and more sparkling, and deeper than other wells; and as they trace the spillings of full pitchers on the heated ground, they snuff the freshness, and, sighing, cast sad looks towards the Thames, and think of baths and boats, and saunter on, despondent."

It is in the Middle Temple where we are introduced to Mr Chester. He is seated in Paper Buildings, which can still be seen.
"It was in a room in Paper Buildings - a row of goodly tenements, shaded in front by ancient trees, and looking, at the back, upon the Temple Gardens - that his, our idler, lounged; now taking up again the paper he had laid down a hundred times; now trifling with the fragments of his meal; now pulling forth his golden toothpick, and glancing leisurely about the room, or out at window into the trim garden walks, where a few early loiterers were already pacing to and fro."

References to the Middle Temple are peppered about the works of Dickens, but perhaps the most memorable of them is made in *Martin Chuzzlewit*, when the author uses Fountain Court [32] as the regular meeting point for Ruth Pinch and her brother, Tom.

The Inns of Court are open to the public during the working week.
Nearest tube for Gray's Inn, Furnival's Inn, Barnard's Inn and Staple Inn: Chancery Lane (Central line).
For Middle Temple: Temple (District and Circle lines).

The Marshalsea
Southwark, SW1.

All that remains of the infamous Marshalsea prison stands in a forgotten corner of a church yard which itself has been converted into a small and depressingly spartan park. Located just north of St George's Church in the Borough, the last vestige of the Marshalsea - a fragment of wall containing the entrance arch - is marked only by a perfunctory plaque put up by the local council.

The absence of any proper information is surprising considering the historic importance of the gaol, however a vivid portrait of conditions in the place is to be found in the works of Charles Dickens. The section of wall that is to be seen today was in fact part of the building that Dickens knew but the Marshalsea prison actually existed long before his day, on a site a short distance away.

The original Marshalsea stood near present-day Mermaid Court, Southwark. It is uncertain when the prison was founded but it must have existed for some time before the Peasants' Revolt as it is known that Wat Tyler's rebels attacked it in 1381. At first the prison was used to confine people found guilty of offences committed within the precincts of the Court but later it became a gaol for pirates, smugglers and others perpetrating crimes at sea.

The Marshalsea grew in importance under Elizabeth I when it was used to imprison both debtors and dissenters. Bonner, who was bishop of London at the time of Elizabeth's accession was incarcerated here for ten years after refusing to take the oath of allegiance. He eventually died in the gaol in 1569 after a further period of detention.

But the Marshalsea wasn't just reserved for prisoners of conscience. Anyone who dared to defy authority could expect to end up there. The poet Christopher Brooke discovered this in 1609 when he was foolish and romantic enough to help his friend John Donne to marry his sweetheart Anne More, without her father's consent.

Another poet who suffered the same fate, though for more serious reasons, was George Wither. Wither, who had been an officer in Cromwell's army, was locked up in 1613 for having written the satire *'Abuses Stript and Whipt'*. This did not seem to affect his creativity, though, for he wrote the poem, *'The Shepherd's Hunting'*, which is generally regarded as his best, whilst in the gaol. He was released some years before his death.

By the eighteenth century, the old Marshalsea had fallen into such a bad state of repair that it was closed. A new gaol was erected nearby, close to St George's Church and it was this prison that Dickens described with such passion in Little Dorrit [28]. Dickens, in fact, had an intimate knowledge of the gaol as his father was imprisoned here for debt in1824. This was one of the author's most painful memories. Aged just 12 at the time, he was put into lodgings by himself and sent to work in a boot blacking factory. The experience, thinly disguised in David Copperfield, haunted him for the rest of his life.

The Marshalsea prison was eventually closed in the late 19th century and demolished sometime afterwards. The district is still redolent with Dickens associations and the visitor will find Marshalsea Road, Dorrit Street, Quilp Street, and of course, Lant Street, the site of Dickens' boyhood lodging.

The remains of the Marshalsea stand in a public park and can be seen at any time during the day.
Nearest tube: London Bridge (Northern Line).

Dickens's House

48, Doughty Street, WC1.

The elegant four-storey house which was home to Charles Dickens and his wife Catherine in the early years of their marriage indicated a step up in the world for the author, who until 1837 had only been able to afford the lease on a cramped apartment in Furnival's Inn. Thanks to the success of *Pickwick Papers*, [20] though, Dickens was suddenly able to pay the £80 per year it took to rent the property. At that time, Doughty Street was a private road with gates at each end as well as its own porters, so Dickens must have felt that he had really arrived when he took up residence.

Although Dickens only spent two years in this house, it was the scene of some of his happiest and saddest moments. A mine of creativity, Dickens managed to write the last chapters of *Pickwick Papers* here and went on to produce *Oliver Twist* [25] and *Nicholas Nickleby*. Just over a month after moving into Doughty Street, though, the author's prolific output was halted by the death of his beloved sister-in-law, Mary Hogarth. Dickens was so shattered by the experience that the publication of both *Pickwick* and *Oliver Twist* had to be temporarily halted.

The last surviving London home of the author, 48, Doughty Street was saved from demolition in 1923 by the Dickens Fellowship. The society has since lovingly restored the building, as far as possible reconstructing the rooms as Dickens might have known them. Inside is a fascinating collection of memorabilia including many of the author's personal belongings. Alongside famous items such as his desk and chair are quills which he wrote with, the pottery monkey he insisted was always in place before he started work and many more possessions ranging from the quirky to the mundane.

Dickens was, of course, universally acclaimed as an author in his own lifetime and most of the exhibits in this fine collection represent the trappings of a man who achieved status and wealth. Despite this, it is clear from his writing that there was something in the private man which never escaped the terrors of the past. The house in Doughty Street now contains two of the most poignant reminders of that time: the tiny wooden window from the attic room Dickens occupied when his parents moved to London from Chatham in 1823 and a grille from the Marshalsea prison, where his father was imprisoned for debt just a year later.

As well as being the headquarters of the Dickens Fellowship, 48, Doughty Street contains the Dickens Library, a comprehensive collection of books and other rare items. There is also an unique collection of manuscripts and an extensive photographic collection. Access to these archives are subject to permission from the Curator and researchers should apply for an appointment.

The Dickens House Museum is open Monday to Saturday, 10 a.m. to 5 p.m. Last admissions 4.30 p.m.

Adults: £5; Children £3;Students/Seniors: £4; Families £14.
Nearest tube: Russell Square (Piccadilly Line).

The Roman Bath

Strand Lane, WC2

Just off the Strand in a narrow back alley is an ancient curiosity known as the Roman Bath. Entirely hidden by the surrounding buildings and with only a polite little sign to guide the way from Surrey Street, it is hardly surprising that the bath goes unnoticed by most. But anyone inquisitive enough to walk a few steps down the strange lane which leads to the site should find the trip rewarding.

A flight of steps opens on to Strand Lane and turning right you can see the old watch house with its wonderfully grim-looking light. The bath can be found just in front of the watch house arch. It is behind some railings on the right hand side and it can be viewed through a large glass window set at street level.

Despite its historical title, the bath is probably not Roman and there is no archaeological evidence to support the name. Nevertheless, it must be more than three centuries old as it is referred to in documents dating from 1784.

The bath - a plunge bath measuring around 13 feet by 6 feet - is contained in a vaulted room enclosed in red brick and it is believed that its feed water comes from the Holy Well of St Clement, nearby, which was once greatly valued for its spa qualities. Now looking rather musty and unloved, the bath was in regular use until quite recently. In the last century, Charles Dickens used to bathe here and he mentions it in chapter thirty-five of *David Copperfield* [16].

Strand Lane, which is believed to follow the bed of a stream which ran from Drury Lane to the Thames, has been effectively cut off from the hubbub of the Strand and Aldwich due to the expansion of Kings College and what remains of it has a vaguely sinister air. It is said that it was in a house in this neighbourhood that Guy Fawkes and his comrades took the oath of secrecy and received the sacrament before setting out the Gunpowder Plot. Looking around this dark and dingy passage, it is easy to believe.

The Roman Bath can be viewed from the street. For closer inspection, it is open to the public by appointment only on Wednesdays from May to the end of September during office hours.
Please telephone: 0207-641-5264 or fax: 0207-641-5215.
There is a small admission charge.
Nearest tube: Temple (District line)

St Mary le Strand

The WRENS' Church

Strand WC2

The graceful baroque church of St Mary le Strand might have been less lovely to look at if Queen Anne had not died in 1714. For at the time of building, St. Mary's was not supposed to have a steeple. Instead, the church was to have a 250 ft high column put up beside it with a statue of the queen on top. When she died and the project was scrapped, St. Mary's got its steeple after all.

Erected between 1714 and 1717, St. Mary le Strand was the work of the architect James Gibbs, whose reputation was made when its beauty and delicacy was widely acclaimed. The church was built to replace a much earlier version which stood a short distance away on the site of Somerset House. Thomas à Becket is said to have been a rector there.

The second St Mary's has several claims to fame of its own, though. A large Maypole once stood on the green outside andalthough the original was destroyed by the Puritans in 1644, a new one was put up during the Restoration, much to the delight of the common folk. This in its turn was taken down in 1718 when it was bought by Sir Isaac Newton to support a telescope.

More than thirty years later, in 1750, St. Mary's is said to have had a clandestine visitor in the shape of Prince Charles Edward, better known as 'Bonnie Prince Charlie'. The Prince allegedly renounced the Catholic faith and was received into the Church of England here during a secret five-day sojourn.

St. Mary le Strand also has a connection with Charles Dickens. According to the church register, his parents, John Dickens and Elizabeth Barrow, were married here on June 13, 1809.

An unusual and interesting church, St. Mary's has unfortunately been cut off from the surrounding streets by London's changing traffic system. This has left it looking rather forlorn on a little island in the middle of the road. But its interior is well worth dodging the taxis and buses to see, in particular it has an elaborate plasterwork ceiling which is best viewed through the mirrors left out at the back of the church.

St. Mary-le-Strand is the official church of the Women's Royal Naval Service, the Women's Royal Naval Reserve and the Association of Wrens. A Book of

Remembrance records the names of members who have died in service from the First World War to the present day.

St. Mary le Strand is open from 11 a.m. to 4 pm. Monday to Friday and from 4 pm. Sunday. Music recitals are given at 1.05 pm. on Wednesdays and Fridays.
No charge is made for entrance or for recitals but donations towards the church's upkeep are welcome, however small.

David Copperfield

David Copperfield is widely acknowledged as the most autobiographical of Dickens's novels and much of the misery of the author's early life is heart-rendingly described in its pages. One of the most enduring and painful recollections that Dickens suffered was that of being sent to work in a blacking (polish) warehouse as a child. The warehouse was situated just off the Strand, on part of the site now occupied by Charing Cross station and this area features strongly in the novel.

In the following section of the book, the place Dickens knew as Warren's Blacking Factory becomes Murdstone & Grinby's wine warehouse.

Chapter 11

'Murdstone and Grinby's warehouse was at the water-side. It was down in Blackfriars. Modern improvements have altered the place; but it was the last house at the bottom of a narrow street, curving down hill to the river, with some stairs and the end, where people took boat. It was a crazy old house with a wharf of its own, abutting on the water when the tide was in, and on the mud when the tide was out and

literally overrun with rats. Its panelled rooms discoloured with the dirt and smoke of a hundred years, I dare say; its decaying floors and staircase; the squeaking and scuffling of the old grey rats down in the cellars; and the dirt and rottenness of the place; are things, not of many years ago, in my mind, but of the present instant. They are all before me, just as they were in the evil hour when I went among them for the first time, with my trembling hand in Mr Quinion's.'

Immediately East of Charing Cross station is a walkway which leads down to Villiers Street. As in Dickens' description, it is a narrow street, curving downhill to the river. Before the Victoria Embankment was built, the river came to a point almost half way up this street. At the end would have been the wooden steps described by the author and, close by, the hated blacking factory. The steps, were known as the Hungerford Stairs and they were then a point of embarkment for emigrants. Again, Dickens cleverly places his fictional characters against a factual backdrop and uses this location for the Micawber family's impending flight to Australia.

<u>Chapter 57</u>

'Thus Traddles and I found them at nightfall, assembled on the wooden steps, at that time known as Hungerford Stairs, watching the departure of a boat with some of their property on board. I had told Traddles of the terrible event, and it had greatly shocked him; but there could be no doubt of the kindness of keeping it a secret, and he had come to help me in this last service. It was here that I took Mr. Micawber aside, and received his promise.

The Micawber family were lodged in a little, dirty,

tumble-down public-house, which in those days was close to the stairs, and whose protruding wooden rooms overhung the river. The family, as emigrants, being objects of some interest in and about Hungerford, attracted so many beholders, that we were glad to take refuge in their room. It was one of the wooden chambers upstairs, with the tide flowing underneath.'

The reader can easily imagine the jumble of decrepit old hostels which then crowded around the Thames shoreline. One of the better known was the Golden Cross inn, which had been around long enough to become a local landmark. It is here that Copperfield and Steerforth are made to stay before going on to Steerforth's home in Highgate.

<u>Chapter 19.</u>

'We went to the Golden Cross, at Charing Cross, then a mouldy sort of establishment in a close neighbourhood. A waiter showed me into the coffee-room; and a chambermaid introduced me to my small bedchamber, which smelt like a hackney-coach, and was shut up like a family vault. I was still painfully conscious of my youth, for nobody stood in any awe of me at all: the chambermaid being utterly indifferent to my opinions on any subject, and the waiter being familiar with me, and offering advice to my inexperience.'

The Golden Cross has long since disappeared, but it used to stand near the corner of the Strand and Whitehall. The view of the statue of King Charles I at that side of Trafalgar Square is described at the beginning of Chapter

20, when Dickens has Copperfield tell how the chambermaid: *'stood peeping out of the window at King Charles on horseback, surrounded by a maze of hackney-coaches, and looking anything but regal in a drizzling rain and a dark-brown fog.'*

Another, and rather happier memory that Dickens refers to in David Copperfield is that of enjoying a cold dip in his favourite bathing pool, which was situated a little further down the Strand. Then as now, the pool was known as the Roman Bath, [11] athough its true date is unknown. The author mentions it in chapter thirty-five:

"There was an old Roman bath in those days at the bottom of one of the streets out of the Strand - it may be there still - in which I have had many a cold plunge. Dressing myself as quietly as I could, and leaving Peggotty to look after my aunt, I tumbled head foremost into it, and then went for a walk to Hampstead. "

There is another brief reference to the bath in Chapter thirty-six.

Pickwick Papers

(The Posthumous Papers of the Pickwick Club)

There were a number of famous coaching inns in the Borough, Southwark, since this was the main London to Canterbury road. Probably the best known of the inns was the Tabard and pilgrims on their way to the tomb of Thomas a Becket used it as a starting point, as was we know from Chaucer's 'Canterbury Tales'. Like the other Borough inns, the Tabard was built around a large courtyard with galleries on three sides. The same style was adopted at the White Hart, the inn at which readers of Pickwick Papers are introduced to Sam Weller. Both the Tabard and the White Hart were demolished in the late nineteenth century but one of their sisters survives not far from London Bridge. The George [12] is the last remaining galleried inn in London and although only one wing of the original three is left standing, there is enough of it to give the onlooker the feel of the place as it was and as the White Hart was, when Dickens wrote the following description.

Chapter 10.

"In the Borough especially, there still remain some half dozen old inns, which have preserved their external features unchanged, and which have escaped alike the rage for public improvement, and the encroachments of private speculation. Great, rambling, queer, old places they are, with galleries, and passages, and staircases, wide enough and antiquated enough to furnish materials for a hundred ghost stories, supposing we should ever be reduced to the lamentable necessity of inventing any, and that the world should exist long enough to exhaust the innumerable veracious legends connected with old London Bridge, and its adjacent neighbourhood on the Surrey side.

It was in the yard of one of these inns - of no less celebrated a one than the White Hart - that a man was busily employed in brushing the dirt off a pair of boots, early on the morning succeeding the events narrated in the last chapter. He was habited in a coarse-striped waistcoat, with black calico sleeves, and blue glass buttons; drab breeches and leggings. A bright red handkerchief was wound in a very loose and unstudied style round his neck, and an old white hat was carelessly thrown on one side of his head. There were two rows of boots before him, one cleaned and the other dirty, and at every addition he made to the clean row, he paused from his work, and contemplated its results with evident satisfaction.

The yard presented none of that bustle and activity which are the usual characteristics of a large coach inn.

Three or four lumbering wagons, each with a pile of goods beneath its ample canopy, about the height of the second-floor window of an ordinary house, were stowed away beneath a lofty roof which extended over one end of the yard; and another, which was probably to commence its journey that morning, was drawn out into the open space. A double tier of bed-room galleries, with old clumsy balustrades, ran round two sides of the straggling area, and a double row of bells to correspond, sheltered from the weather by a little sloping roof, hung over the door leading to the bar and coffee-room. Two or three gigs and chaise-carts were wheeled up under different little sheds and pent-houses; and the occasional heavy tread of a cart-horse, or rattling of a chain at the further end of the yard, announced to anybody who cared about the matter, that the stable lay in that direction. When we add that a few boys in smock frocks were lying asleep on heavy packages, woolpacks, and other articles that were scattered about on heaps of straw, we have described as fully as need be the general appearance of the yard of the White Hart Inn, High Street, Borough, on the particular morning in question."

Some of the black and battered balusters which supported the 'clumsy balustrade' mentioned here were rescued when the White Hart was demolished and can now be seen in the basement of Dicken's House Museum [8]. Dickens was a passionate critic of the injustices of his day and he used his novels to drive home his message. He was particularly incensed about the unequal treatment dealt out to the poor who, on top of other miseries, frequently found themselves imprisoned for debt. Two of London's most notorious debtor's prisons were the Fleet and the

Marshalsea [5] and both are described in Pickwick Papers. The Fleet prison was demolished in 1844 but Dickens gives a vivid picture of its latter days when he has Pickwick imprisoned there for several months after an action for debt is taken against him by his landlady, Mrs Bardell.

<u>Chapter 41</u>

"This," said the gentleman, thrusting his hands into his pockets, and looking carelessly over his shoulder to Mr. Pickwick, "This here is the hall flight."

"Oh," replied Mr. Pickwick, looking down a dark and filthy staircase, which appeared to lead to a range of damp and gloomy stone vaults, beneath the ground, "and those, I suppose, are the little cellars where the prisoners keep their small quantities of coals. Unpleasant places to have to go down to; but very convenient, I dare say."

"Yes, I shouldn't wonder if they was convenient," replied the gentleman, "seeing that a few people live there, pretty snug. That's the Fair, that is."

"My friend," said Mr. Pickwick, "you don't really mean to say that human beings live down in those wretched dungeons?"

"Don't I?" replied Mr. Roker, with indignant astonishment; "why shouldn't I?"

"Live! Live down there!" exclaimed Mr. Pickwick.

"Live down there! Yes, and die down there, too, wery often!" replied Mr. Roker; "and what of that? Who's got to say anything agin it? Live down there! Yes, and a wery good place it is to live in, ain't it?"

Conditions at the infamous Marshalsea Prison, which

features so strongly in *Little Dorrit*, are described in a similarly lurid way when Dickens relates The Old Man's Tale About The Queer Client in Chapter 21.

"In the Borough High Street, near Saint George's Church, and on the same side of the way, stands, as most people know, the smallest of our debtors' prisons, the Marshalsea. Although in later times it has been a very different place from the sink of filth and dirt it once was, even its improved condition holds out but little temptation to the extravagant, or consolation to the improvident.

The condemned felon has as good a yard for air and exercise in Newgate, as the insolvent debtor in the Marshalsea Prison.

"It may be my fancy, or it may be that I cannot separate the place from the old recollections associated with it, but this part of London I cannot bear. The street is broad, the shops are spacious, the noise of passing vehicles, the footsteps of a perpetual stream of people - all the busy sounds of traffic, resound in it from morn to midnight, but the streets around are mean and close; poverty and debauchery lie festering in the crowded alleys; want and misfortune are pent up in the narrow prison; an air of gloom and dreariness seems, in my eyes at least, to hang about the scene, and to impart to it a squalid and sickly hue."

Oliver Twist

London Bridge as it crosses into Southwark was the setting chosen by Dickens for Nancy's fateful rendezvous with Rose Mayew and Mr Brownlow. Not knowing that she has been followed, she innocently meets the couple at midnight on the steps leading to the Surrey Pier and gives them crucial information about Oliver's whereabouts. The author gives a chilling account of the kindness that was to cause her death.

<u>Chapter 46</u>

"The church clocks chimed three quarters past eleven, as two figures emerged on London Bridge. One, which advanced with a swift and rapid step, was that of a woman who looked eagerly about her as though in quest of some expected object; the other figure was that of a man, who slunk along in the deepest shadow he could find, and, at some distance, accommodated his pace to hers; stopping when she stopped; and as she moved again, creeping stealthily on: but never allowing himself, in the ardour of his pursuit, to gain upon her footsteps. Thus, they crossed the bridge, from the Middlesex to the Surrey shore, when the

woman, apparently disappointed in her anxious scrutiny of the foot passengers, turned back. The movement was sudden: but he who watched her, was not thrown off his guard by it; for, shrinking into one of the recesses which surmount the piers of the bridge, and leaning over the parapet the better to conceal his figure, he suffered her to pass on the opposite pavement. When she was about the same distance in advance as she had been before, he slipped quietly down and followed her again. At nearly the centre of the bridge, she stopped. The man stopped too.
It was a very dark night. The day had been unfavourable, and at that hour and place there were few people stirring. Such as there were hurried quickly past; very possibly without seeing, but certainly without noticing, either the woman, or the man who kept her in view. Their appearance was not calculated to attract the importunate regards of such of London's destitute population, as chanced to take their way over the bridge that night in search of some cold arch or door-less hovel wherein to lay their heads; they stood there in silence: neither speaking nor spoken to, by any one who passed.

A mist hung over the river, deepening the red glare of the fires that burnt upon the small craft moored off the different wharves, and rendering darker and more indistinct the murky buildings on the banks. The old smoke-stained storehouses on either side, rose heavy and dull from the dense mass of roofs and gables, and frowned sternly upon the water too black to reflect even their lumbering shapes. The tower of old Saint Saviour's Church, and the spire of Saint Magnus, so long the giant-warders of the ancient bridge, were visible in the gloom; but the forest of shipping below the bridge, and the thickly scattered spires of churches above, were nearly all hidden from the sight."

St. Saviour's church was Southwark Cathedral, [8] one of the great hidden gems of the city.

Southwark Cathedral

Little Dorrit

The story of Little Dorrit plays out in and around the Marshalsea prison, [5] one of London's best known gaols and one with which Dickens was well acquainted, since his father spent some months incarcerated there for debt. The prison, which, unusually, was very much like a village behind bars, had been shut down by the time the author came to write Little Dorrit but relics of it remained. He describes how it looked when he returned on a research trip in his preface to the book:

"I found the outer front courtyard metamorphosed into a butter-shop; and I then almost gave up every brick of the jail for lost. Wandering, however, down a certain adjacent 'Angel Court, leading to Bermondsey', I came to Marshalsea Place, the houses in which I recognised, not only as the great block of the former prison, but as preserving the rooms that arose to my mind's eye when I became Little Dorrit's biographer...Whosoever goes into Marshalsea Place, turning out of Angel Court leading to Bermondsey, will find his feet on the very paving-stones of the extinct Marshalsea jail; will see its narrow yard to the right and to the left, very little altered if at all, except that

the walls were lowered when the place got free; will look upon the rooms in which the debtors lived; will stand among the crowding ghosts of many miserable years."

All that is left of the Marshalsea today stands in the remnant of St George's Church yard where a simple and uninformative plaque put up by the council does little to commemorate the spot. The church itself can also still be seen, although it is hopelessly cut off by a busy road loop. Inside it is the font where Dickens has Little Dorrit baptised, the altar where he has her married and the vestry where he makes her sleep, with the burial-book for a pillow.

St. George's Church, Southwark

Martin Chuzzlewit

According to Dickens, the amiable Tom Pinch has his 'solitary office' in Middle Temple - a place well-known to the author and mentioned in several novels. He describes the chambers where Tom is to be a secretary and librarian for a mystery employer in a very enigmatic way.

<u>Chapter 40</u>

"There was a ghostly air about these uninhabited chambers in the Temple, and attending every circumstance of Tom's employment there, which had a strange charm in it. Every morning when he shut his door at Islington, he turned his face towards an atmosphere of unaccountable fascination, as surely as he turned it to the London smoke; and from that moment it thickened round and round him all day long, until the time arrived for going home again, and leaving it, like a motionless cloud, behind.

It seemed to Tom, every morning, that he approached this ghostly mist, and became enveloped in it, by the easiest succession of degrees imaginable. Passing from the roar and rattle of the streets into the quiet court-yards of the

Temple, was the first preparation. Every echo of his footsteps sounded to him like a sound from the old walls and pavements, wanting language to relate the histories of the dim, dismal rooms; to tell him what lost documents were decaying in forgotten corners of the shut-up cellars, from whose lattices such mouldy sighs came breathing forth as he went past; to whisper of dark bins of rare old wine bricked up in vaults among the old foundations of the Halls; or mutter in a lower tone yet darker legends of the cross-legged knights, whose marble effigies were in the church. With the first planting of his foot upon the staircase of his dusty office, all these mysteries increased; until, ascending step by step, as Tom ascended, they attained their full growth in the solitary labours of the day.'

Set at the heart of Middle Temple, Tom's office is a short step away from a secluded courtyard where a single jet fountain bubbles gently among the trees. The courtyard, known as Fountain Court, becomes Tom's rendezvous with his sister, Ruth.

Chapter 45

"There was a little plot between them, that Tom should always come out of the Temple by one way; and that was past the fountain. Coming through Fountain Court, he was just to glance down the steps leading into Garden Court, and to look once all round him; and if Ruth had come to meet him, there he would see her; not sauntering, you understand (on account of the clerks), but coming briskly up, with the best little laugh upon her face that ever played in opposition to the fountain, and beat it all to nothing."

Later in the novel, Ruth walks to Fountain Court on the arm of John Westlock.

Chapter 53

"Brilliantly the Temple Fountain sparkled in the sun, and laughingly its liquid music played, and merrily the idle drops of water danced and danced, and, peeping out in sport among the trees, plunged lightly down to hide themselves, as little Ruth and her companion came towards it."

Fountain Court

Fountain Court has lost none of its charm and tranquility to this day.

Hidden London

The American Connection

The American Connection

Many of America's founding fathers sailed from England hoping to find their fortunes or their freedom in the New World. Whether they were adventurers, pioneers or pilgrims, these early colonists left links to their origins behind, particularly in London's city churches.

For easy reference, the contents listing overleaf has been set out colony by colony with the names of the relevant sites and the founding fathers associated with them given below. Opposite, the locations are listed by name and page number.

The U.S. flag will guide you to particular points of interest.

Contents

Contents

All Hallows, Barking

Byward Street, EC3

Of the thousands who flock to the Tower of London every year, very few notice the modest-looking church which stands only a few feet away. Yet despite its post-war appearance, All Hallows actually predates the Tower by 400 years.

Rising on Saxon foundations and nestling between fifteenth-century walls, the modern All Hallows is all too easily dismissed at first glance - even the interior seems unremarkable. For the historic remains of the church have been so carefully incorporated into the reconstruction that it takes time to discover them all.

With its odd mix of architecture and even odder name (it was founded on land belonging to the abbey at Barking, Essex) All Hallows is an elegant eccentric. Remodelled and rebuilt several times over the centuries, the church maintains an unbroken tradition of religious ritual. There was a place of worship here long before the dawn of Christianity and the English Druidical Order still gathers here for its ceremonies.

At the commercial hub of the city and with commanding views of the Thames, All Hallows has always been an important church. Its status was assured by its links with the Port of London and increased as Britain became a major maritime force.

This special bond with the seafaring community has given All Hallows a distinctive flavour. In fact one of the first things a visitor notices is that there are models of ships everywhere - hanging in the arches, nestling in the window ledges, attached to walls - all lovingly constructed and beautifully detailed.

The models, part of a collection which is unique in British churches, are tokens of thanks for cargoes safely delivered and voyages completed unscathed. Today they serve as a pertinent reminder of how perilous sea journeys were when men navigated by the stars.

While all of the ships on display have their interest, the three most notable models are that of the Santa Maria, located above the gallery door, which is the earliest; that next to it, an elaborate model of the Victory and that of the TSMV Royal Daffodil, which can be seen in a glass case by the stairs. The last, a comparatively recent donation, will strike a particular chord with those who served in the Second World War, as she was one the flotilla of little ships which helped evacuate troops from Dunkirk in 1940.

The Mariners' Chapel in the South Aisle has more evidence of All Hallows' long relationship with the sea. The focal point of the Chapel's screen is a crucifix made of wood that came from the Cutty Sark bearing an ivory figure of Christ which is said to have come from the flagship of the Spanish Armada.

When the docks handled millions of tons of merchandise and the river was a forest of masts, All Hallows was strategically placed to serve state officials as well as ordinary sailors. The Custom House and the Navy Office were both within its parish boundary and this was its saviour in the 17th century when the Great Fire cut a swathe through the city.

The head of the Navy Office at that time was Admiral General Sir William Penn who also happened to live nearby. The Admiral's desperate bid to head off the blaze was recorded by his friend and trusted colleague, Samuel Pepys. In his diary for Wednesday September 5, 1666, Pepys noted: *'But going to the fire, I find, by the blowing up of houses and the great help given by the workmen out of the King's yards, sent up by Sir W Penn, there is a good stop given to it.'* Later, however, he added: *'I up to the top of Barkeing steeple, and there saw the saddest sight of desolation that I ever saw...* '

Barkeing steeple was, of course, the tower of All Hallows. The tower survived to look out over a similar scene of devastation when the Blitz destroyed the city almost three hundred years later. Unfortunately, though, the unspoilt medieval church did not.

By a miracle, some marvellous relics have been preserved nonetheless. One, a magnificent Saxon arch, the largest artefact of the era to be found anywhere in London, came to light when a bomb blast blew down the wall which was covering it. The arch, which contains Roman tiles, stands over the site of a second-century house and part of the floor of that house is a prize exhibit in the small museum of local history which has been set up in the undercroft.

Also in the undercroft are the church registers - an unmissable sight, as much for their antiquity as for the chance of catching a glimpse of the many famous names they contain. Since the records date from the reign of Elizabeth I, one name not included is that of Bishop John Fisher, who was executed on Tower Hill in 1535 and interred near the North Porch. Fisher, who first opposed Henry VIII's divorce from Catherine of Aragon and then refused to accept the King as head of the church, is remembered instead in a sculpture over the porch entrance. His remains were later transferred to St Peter Ad Vincula, on Tower Green.

A victim of political intrigue who does feature in the register, though, is William Laud who was Archbishop of Canterbury to Charles I and his prime supporter against Parliament. Laud was finally trapped and beheaded in 1644 and the word 'Traitor' can been seen smeared out next to the entry in the book of burials. The bishop's body was later removed to St John's College, Oxford.

The year 1644 saw another significant event at the church, especially for American history. On October 23, the same William Penn who was to save All Hallows from the Great Fire brought his baby son to be baptised here. So *'William, son of William Penn and Margaret his wife, of the Tower Liberty'* was taken into the church that he would later reject in favour of theQuaker faith. Penn [29] [8], whose relentless search for religious freedom led to the founding of Pennsylvania, was christened in the existing baptistery although the wooden font which was then in use is now in Christ Church, Philadelphia. A fabulous font cover, believed to be the work of Grinling Gibbons, protects the present stone font. Of marriages recorded at All Hallows, one of the most interesting is that of John Quincy Adams, later sixth president of the United States, which took place in 1797. In England to help resolve important political issues Adams obviously still made time for romance!

A much more unlikely romantic to tie the knot at All Hallows was George Jeffryes, afterwards the notorious 'hanging judge'. He married his first wife, Sarah Neesham, here in 1667.

All Hallows is open Monday to Friday 9am - 6pm. Saturdays & Sundays from 10am - 5pm. The Crypt Museum is open Monday to Friday & on Saturdays from 11am - 4pm. On Sundays, it is open after the service from around 1.30pm - 4pm. Entrance is free.

A free audio tour of the church and the museum is also available but you are asked to make a suggested donation of £2.50.

Group tours can be arranged by contacting the Verger on: 0207-481-2928.

Nearest tube: Tower Hill (District & Circle lines)

St. Bride's

(The Printers' Church)
Fleet Street, EC4

The churchyard of St. Bride's is now best known to office workers who come to share their lunchtime snacks with grubby but appealing city sparrows. Just a few steps from the noise and bustle of Fleet Street, the churchyard is dark and surprisingly silent. Yet for centuries, it was the hub of the publishing industry and generations of British writers from Shakespeare to Dickens knew it intimately.

St. Bride's connection with the print trade dates back almost 500 years. William Caxton's apprentice, Wynkyn de Worde, brought England's first moveable-type press to the churchyard in 1535. de Worde's best customers were the clergy, who were the most literate group of the time but soon playwrights, poets and pamphleteers were racing to the publisher and rival presses quickly set up in competition in nearby churchyards.

The press soon became a force to be reckoned with and, thanks to de Worde, Fleet Street was its centre. Great writers flocked to live in the surrounding streets just to be close to their publishers. Dryden and Milton lodged within a few hundred yards of St. Bride's, as did the poet Lovelace, who was buried at the church. The famous diarist, Pepys, was born in nearby Axe Lane and was baptised in the church. His contemporary, Evelyn, lived a short distance away in Fetter Lane, which was in the same parish.

As its literary links flourished, Fleet Street became a meeting place for intellectuals. Samuel Johnson, Boswell, Goldsmith, Burke and Pope were familiar figures around St. Bride's as were two of the eighteenth century's most popular artists, Joshua Reynolds and William Hogarth [27].

The church of St. Bride's has stood on the same plot of London soil for 1500 years. Named in honour of St. Bridget of Kildare, Ireland, the first known stone building was erected on the site in the sixth century, probably by a community of local Celts. By Norman times, St. Bride's had become a prominent city church. The Curia Regis met here in 1205 and King John held a parliament here in 1210.

No fewer than eight buildings dedicated to St. Bride have occupied this position over the centuries, the latest a restoration of Sir Christopher Wren's church of 1675. Itself a reconstruction following the Great Fire of London, Wren's church was destroyed again in the Blitz. All that remains of his work today is the magnificent steeple and, on the interior, the minstrel's gallery incorporated into its base.

The steeple, though, has endured as a landmark not only in London but nation-wide. When an enterprising Fleet Street baker made a copy of Wren's tower in the shape of a multi-tiered wedding cake, he started a fashion which has endured for almost three hundred years.

But this is only one of the steeple's claims to fame. Originally the tallest of Wren's church spires, it stood a lofty 234 feet until lightening struck in 1764. This unfortunate incident not only reduced the structure by eight feet but sparked off a row of spectacular proportions between King George III and the American scientist and philosopher, Benjamin Franklin [32] [4]. Renowned for his experiments with electricity, Franklin was called in to advise the King on the question of lightening rods. Franklin recommended conductors with pointed ends but the King argued in favour of blunt ones. Political pamphleteers had a field day with the resulting controversy, delighting in references to *'good, blunt, honest King George'* and *'those sharp-witted colonists.'*

St. Bride's had, in fact, figured strongly in the history of those same colonists for some two hundred years by then. The parents of Virginia Dare, the first child born to English emigrants to North Carolina in 1587, were married at the church. The event is commemorated in a touching bust of a little girl, which is made all the more poignant for the fact that Virginia was fated to disappear along with other members of Raleigh's Lost Colony. The bust can be found by the font.

One of the most striking features of modern-day St.

Bride's also owes its inspiration to the church's American links. The great free-standing canopied oak reredos which enshrines the church altar is a memorial to the Pilgrim Fathers [35] [7].

This connection was made thirty-three years after Virginia Dare's birth when Edward Winslow (1595 - 1655) became one of the leaders of the Mayflower expedition. Winslow, who was elected Governor of Plymouth, Massachusetts three times, served as a boy apprentice in Fleet Street and would have known St. Bride's well. His parents were also married there.

In the same timescale, St. Bride's parish was busily helping to populate yet another English colony. One hundred girls and boys from the Bridewell Hospital orphanage were sent to Virginia in 1619. The project was so successful that the governor requested a hundred more. All the youngsters received grants of land on coming of age.

As well as contributing to the historical heritage of the American nation, St. Bride's has had considerable significance at home too. After wartime bombing reduced the church to a shell, archaeologists found a Roman pavement and the remains of a Roman house while excavating the crypt. The foundations of each previous church on the site were also discovered, providing invaluable information.

The dig revealed more gristly finds, of course. Although the burial sections had long been sealed up, the crypt contained thousands of human remains, many of whichwould have belonged to victims of the Great Plague of 1665 and the cholera epidemic of 1854.

Today, though, St. Bride's crypt is anything but

forbidding. Visitors can now explore the undercroft and see the ancient foundations and Roman remains as well as other interesting finds, such as a lockable iron coffin which was used in an attempt to frustrate body snatchers during the eighteenth century.

As the Printers' Church, St. Bride's would not be true to its tradition without a tribute to the trade. An exhibition chronicling the church's close association with the press is on permanent display in the crypt.

• Materials on all aspects of books and printing plus many archives and artefacts can be found close by at the St. Bride Printing Library, Bride Lane. It is open Monday to Friday, 9.30 am. - 5.30 pm.

St. Bride's is open weekdays from 8am - 4.45pm. Saturdays 10am - 3pm. Sunday Services at 11am & 6.30pm. No charge is made to either the church or the crypt museum but donations are welcome.

Nearest tube: Blackfriars (District line).

St. Dunstan-in-the-West

Centre of Prayer for Christian Unity

Fleet Street, EC4.

The pace of city living on any normal work day descends like a cloak, distracting attention from many of London's most interesting buildings. The church of St. Dunstan's in Fleet Street is one of those which fades into the background, its magnificent outline all but obscured by an endless stream of traffic.

To the casual onlooker, St. Dunstan's is just another grimy Victorian Gothic facade jumbled in with the architectures of other ages. The enormous and unusual clock which has become its best-known feature, hardly looks as though it belongs with the building at all.

Once a commanding presence at the entrance of the city's Square Mile, St. Dunstan's has almost shrunk from view, yet it still occupies a privileged position in history. For the name of St. Dunstan's is linked with some of the greatest names in world literature. Donne, Milton, Pepys and Walton were all firmly connected to the church while others such as Shakespeare and Jonson did their business and drank so close by that they were almost certainly visitors.

In more religious times, St. Dunstan's was famed as much for its preachers as its poets. One of these was William Tyndale (1494-1536), whose unauthorised translations of Bible texts ultimately formed the basis of all following versions. By the 17th century, preaching had become something of an art form and many of the best speakers came to St. Dunstan's, drawing massive crowds. A certain cleric, dubbed Dr. 'Silver-tongued' Bates, attracted so many listeners that the audience would pour out of the church doors and overflow into the street. Pepys records going twice in one day to hear Dr. Bates give his last sermon, having to push his way through the throng both times. In his diary for August 17, 1662, he complains that although he got into the gallery beside the pulpit, he: '... stood in a crowd and did exceedingly sweat all the while.'

To walk into St. Dunstan's, today, is a very different experience but one which is powerfully moving, nonetheless. For in entering the church, the visitor crosses the threshold into many cultures of Christianity - a fact immediately brought home by the strikingly beautiful Romanian icon screen which stands to the left of the main altar. Here, alone in the whole of the country, the traditions of the seven major churches of Christendom - that is the Old Catholics, the Assyrian Church of the East, the Romanian

Orthodox Church, the Anglican Church, the Oriental churches, the Lutheran and Reformed Churches and the Holy Roman and Catholic Church - are honoured in four chapels and three shrines set around the octagonal walls.

This eclectic mixture of influences comes as something of a shock, since neither the outer nor inner architecture of the church gives any clue to its exotic contents. Quietly, though, the story of St. Dunstan's has changed. Designated as a centre of prayer for Christian Unity in 1960, it now plays a major role in fostering good relations with churches outside the Anglican communion.

Long before such religious divisions existed in England, though, St. Dunstan's stood at the heart of Fleet Street, a large and imposing structure that originally jutted out thirty feet into the road. Like most churches, St. Dunstan's started small but gradually sprawled over the centuries as chapels and other embellishments were added. The first official record of a church on the site dates to 1185 but it had probably already been in existence for a century by then as Dunstan, a tenth century Archbishop of Canterbury, was consecrated in 1070.

St. Dunstan was the patron saint of goldsmiths, jewellers and locksmiths and he was usually depicted standing at his anvil, a large pair of smith's tongs in hand, threatening to tweak the devil's nose. This was a popular image and was often used on pub signs in the city. A particularly famous example was the pub which stood opposite St. Dunstan's church until 1788. Starting life as 'The Devil and St. Duntan's', the tavern quickly became known as the 'Devil' and it was here that the Apollo Club - a dining club founded and frequented by a string of famous figures - held its meetings. Over the years, members of the club included William Shakespeare, Ben Jonson, Jonathan

Swift, Oliver Goldsmith and Dr. Samuel Johnson [24] amongst many others.

While the 'Devil' counted some of the finest literary talents amongst its customers, the church of St. Dunstan's claimed others in its clergy and congregation. The poet and divine, John Donne, was rector here from 1624 until his death in 1631, holding this office while also Dean of St. Paul's Ludgate, which was one of the main gates into London. Before its demolition in 1760, the Ludgate also featured statues of the legendary pre-Roman King Lud and his two sons. These statues can also be seen at St. Dunstan's but are only found by walking to the right of the church and peering into the vestry porch. Here, looking very time-worn and abandoned, the figures huddle behind a small iron railing.

As well as these having its share of unique monuments on the outside, St. Dunstan's keeps others of equal interest inside the body of the church. There is a bust of John Donne on the east side of the porch. Izaac Walton is remembered in both a plaque on the main entrance and a stained-glass window which was installed in 1895. Although the window is now obscured by the icon screen, it is willingly shown to visitors by the priest on duty. There are also a number of noteworthy memorial stones. This sad little epitaph mourns the passing, in 1679, of one Alexander Layton, a famous swordsman of the day:

> *'His thrusts like lightning flew, more skilful Death*
> *Parried 'em all, and beat him out of breath.'*

Another praises a certain Hobson Judkin, a solicitor so honest that his clients paid for a special stone to be erected following his demise in 1812. A third eulogy remembers the faithful service of Sir Richard Hoare, a former Lord Mayor.

The verse cryptically refers to an 'alarming Crisis' in which he 'discharged the great Trust reposed in him with Honour and Integrity.. ' This is a reference to the crisis caused when news that Charles Edward Stuart, otherwise Bonnie Prince Charlie, and his army had beaten government forces at Prestonpans (1745) and were pressing South. Panic broke out in London as the rumour spread that King George II was preparing to flee the city. Sir Richard, evidently, kept the situation under control until more troops could be mustered and sent to turn back the advancing Scots. Evidence of Sir Richard's readiness for action can now be seen in the form of an impressive sword rest, dated 1745, which stands beside the seat reserved for the Lord Mayor in the front right-hand pew of the church.

These and many other mementoes that help give a glimpse into St. Dunstan's historic past can be easily seen, yet more are hidden from view. The church records are not on show but these contain a wealth of detail, especially for those tracing the trail of America's founding fathers. Perhaps the most exciting are the references to ancestors of the country's first president, George Washington. The entries record the baptism of two of the children of Lawrence Washington junior: a daughter, Anne in 1621 and a son, Lawrence in 1622. Another son, also called Lawrence, had been buried here in 1617. The name Lawrence was obviously important to the family and it was handed down the generations. George Washington's half-brother later inherited the name.

A name which was to become a landmark on the American map also features in St. Dunstan's registers. It is that of Thomas West, Baron de la Warre, who married

Cecilia, daughter of Sir Thomas Shirley here in 1596. Both the proprietor of the Virginia Company and Virginia's first governor, de la Warre's became immortalised in giving his surname to Delaware Bay, river and state.

Another connection to America's first colonists is found through George Calvert, the first Lord Baltimore, who was buried in St. Dunstan's in 1632. Baltimore promoted the charter for the foundation of Maryland and Charles II finally granted it to his son, Cecil. Cecil became the first proprietor of Maryland and installed his brother, Leonard as first governor. Both are remembered in the church of St. Giles-in-the-fields [17], where Cecil was later buried.

- A tablet in memory of Daniel Brown of Connecticut, who was the first Anglican clergyman ordained for America in 1723 is set into the North West alcove of the church.

St. Dunstan-in-the-West is open for worship every day. There is no charge to view the church but donations towards its upkeep are welcome.

Nearest tube: Blackfriars or Temple (District & Circle line).

St. Giles in the Fields

St. Giles High Street, WC2

The name of St. Giles was always associated with lepers and the first building to be erected on the site of the present church was a hospital for sufferers of the disease. The hospital was founded in 1101 by Queen Matilda who was not only the wife of Henry I, but the granddaughter of King Duncan I of Scotland - the same Duncan whose gristly murder by Macbeth was later immortalised by Shakespeare.

Being a leper house, St. Giles was built in the fields which surrounded old London. Today, of course, only the name of the location survives but it serves to differentiate the church from others dedicated to the Saint in the city.

At the outset, St. Giles was no more than a chapel attached to the leper's hospital and it was the custom for prisoners passing the chapel door on their way to execution at Tyburn to be given a 'parting cup' of a bowl of ale as an act of charity. The custom continued long after the chapel became a parish church in 1547.

Thanks to its connections with lepers, prisoners and other social outcasts, the parish of St Giles gained a bad reputation. This was made a great deal worse when the Great Plague of 1665 started within its boundaries. More than 3,000 people died of plague in St. Giles alone, although there were fewer than 2,000 houses in the parish at that time. Samuel Pepys recorded the start of the outbreak in his diary on June 7, 1665: *'This day much against my will I did in Drury Lane see two or three houses marked with a red cross upon the doors, and 'Lord have mercy upon us' writ there, which was a sad sight to me being the first of the kind that to my remembrance I ever saw.'*

But the plague was only one of the horrors to which St. Giles stood witness during its long and often sad history. In 1417 Sir John Oldcastle, the Lollard leader was hung and burnt for treason and heresy not far from the gate. His crime: wanting an English translation of the Bible. Oldcastle was considered a martyr by John Foxe, the Puritan divine, and others.

The church has associations with other religious witch hunts, too. Between 1678 and 1681 no less than 12 Catholics martyrs were buried in St. Giles after Titus Oates claimed that he had discovered a 'Popish Plot' to murder Charles II and restore Catholicism as the state religion. Those executed included the Blessed Oliver Plunket, Archbishop of Armagh, though his body was later exhumed.

Through these events and down the turbulent

centuries, St. Giles-in-the-Fields nonetheless continued to serve the community much like any other parish church and many notable births, marriages and deaths are recorded in its registers. John Milton's daughter, Mary, was baptised here in 1647; the actor David Garrick married Eva Maria Violetti here in 1786; Frances Kemble, the actress also married here in 1786. Lord Byron's daughter, Allegra, and two of Shelley's children were all baptised together at a ceremony in the church in 1818 and the architect John Soane [17] was buried here in 1837.

Of the monuments and memorials to be found at St. Giles, two of the most interesting are to the poets Andrew Marvell and George Chapman. Marvell, whose works have been compared to those of Milton, was buried here in 1678. According to the antiquary John Aubrey (1626-97) his grave is: *'under ye pewes in ye south aisle of St Giles' Church.'* The tomb of George Chapman, who died in1634, is in the churchyard but the tombstone has been removed for safekeeping and now stands the left of the altar at the front of the church. A noted scholar, Chapman was the translator of Homer's '*Iliad*' and of Hesiod's *'Works and Days'*.

Of particular interest to American visitors is a plaque at the back of the church, in memory of Cecilius Calvert, second Lord Baltimore, who is buried here.Baltimore (1606-1675) was the first proprietor of Maryland, having been granted a charter from Charles I. The plaque records that Baltimore's brother, Leonard Calvert, sailed from England with 200 colonists in two ships called the *'Ark* 'and the *'Dove'*. The ships arrived at the Potomac River on 25th March 1634.

In 1671, the cartographer John Ogilby wrote of the colony: : *'Every person who repaireth thither intending to become an inhabitant finds himself secure as well as in the quiet enjoyment of property as of his conscience.'*

The church of St. Giles that we see today opened 1734 and apart from some alterations to the interior, the building has hardly changed. One of the first preachers in the church was John Wesley, who had a chapel in nearby West Street. The top portion of the pulpit from that chapel now stands in the north aisle. Wesley and his brother Charles used it for over 40 years.

St. Giles-in-the-Fields is normally open Monday to Friday 10am - 4pm. Weekday service: Wednesday 1pm. Sunday Services 8am, 11am, 12noon & 6.30pm.

There is no entrance charge.

Nearest tube: Tottenham Court Road

(Central and Northern lines).

St Mary le Bow

Cheapside, EC2.

The Church of St Mary le Bow was one of the first re-buildings erected by Sir Christopher Wren after the Great Fire of London in 1666. Its massive steeple, a square tower surmounted by four stories which reaches 235 feet into the sky, is a well-known landmark in the City, topped as it is by a weather vane in the shape of a sinuous golden dragon .

Wren's solid-looking structure was raised on the site of what was already a very ancient church. As far back as the reign of William the Conqueror, the church of St Mary was known as 'St Marie de Arcubus or Le Bow' because of its arches of stone. And so the name has come down to us to this day.

Perhaps one of the most famous features of St Mary-le-Bow is its bells. These are the bells that a poor runaway boy is said to have heard as he was resting on Highgate milestone when they called: *'Turn again, Whittington, Lord Mayor of London.'* And popular folklore still maintains that only Londoners born within the sound of Bow Bells have the right to call themselves Cockneys.

An interesting historical feature of St Mary's is the balcony in front of the tower. This is a memorial to an incident in 1331 when a wooden balcony, containing Queen Philippa and her ladies, fell during a tournament which was being held to celebrate the birth of the new heir to the throne. This was Edward, later known as the Black Prince.

The balcony continued to be used as a vantage point, despite this mishap, and the Henrys and Edwards came to watch all the great city pageants from here. After Wren rebuilt the church, Queen Anne saw the Lord Mayor's pageant from the balcony in 1702. It was the final display to be devised by the last official City poet.

Another and more famous poet to be associated with the church of St. Mary le Bow is John Milton, who was born in nearby Bread Street. A crumbling plaque on the exterior wall of the church commemorates this fact. As was common in those days, Milton frequently published his works from church yards in Fleet Street. The best-known of these, *'Paradise Lost'* was published from St. Dunstan's, Fleet Street [15].

This was the district where boot makers worked in goatskin leather. The leather was known as Cordovan and the workers as cordwainers. A statue of Captain John Smith (1580 - 1631)

[27][11], a cordwainer who rose to become Governor of Virginia and Admiral of New England, was therefore appropriately placed here.

St. Mary-le-Bow is open Monday to Thursday 7.30am - 6pm and Friday 7.30am. - 3.30pm. The church is not open at weekends.

Nearest tube: Bank or St. Paul's (Central line)

St Sepulchre's

Holborn Viaduct, EC1

The sight of St. Sepulchre's must have chilled the souls of passers-by for several centuris , for it stood opposite the infamous Newgate prison and its bell marked the time of impending executions.

This connection between the church and the prison gave rise to other customs, too. While some of the condemned were executed within the jail, others were hauled off to Tyburn and every death cart would stop outside St. Sepulchre's while the prisoners were presented with a nosegay.

For almost 140 years, though, there was a rather more ghoulish tradition. As the result of a bequest made to St. Sepulchre's in 1605, a bellman was employed to go through a tunnel which connected the church to Newgate on the night before any execution. After giving 'twelve solemn towles with double strokes' on his handbell, he would recite:

"All you that in the condemned hold do lie,
Prepare you, for tomorrow you shall die;
Watch all and pray, the hour is drawing near
That you before the Almighty must appear;
Examine well yourselves, in time repent,
That you may not to eternal flames be sent:
And when St. Sepulchre's bell tomorrow tolls,
The Lord above have mercy on your souls.
Past twelve o'clock!"

These customs died out and Newgate was finally demolished in 1902 to make way for the Old Bailey but the handbell - which can only have added to the desperate misery of the jail's inhabitants - can still be seen in a case on one of the pillars in the church.

Despite these gloomy associations, St. Sepulchre's is an awe-inspiring church with an interior that has all the majestic beauty of a cathedral. None of this would be guessed from the outside, though, since several restorations have robbed the 15th century walls and tower of their original shape. The entrance porch with its remarkable fan tracery roof has fortunately escaped alteration and is the first real clue to the church's historic past.

Founded in 1137, St. Sepulchre's was formerly dedicated to St. Edmund. It's position just outside the north-west gate of the city not only made it a useful starting point for crusaders, it also mirrored that of the Church of the Holy Sepulchre in Jerusalem. These associations led to the church's rededication during the 15th century.

So the Church of the Holy Sepulchre without Newgate, to give it its full title, became firmly established as an important city church. Although the Great Fire of London left the building a shell, the church was quickly rebuilt on its original foundations and some of the mediaeval masonry survived. One interesting relic from the old church is a stone basin or *piscina* which is set into the West wall at the point where the rood screen would have separated the nave and chancel. The scorch marks on the stone are scars from the blaze.

Ironically, the Great Fire stopped suddenly only a few yards away from St. Sepulchre's and it is worth turning into Giltspur Street to see the curious monument that was put up to mark the spot. High on the wall of the modern office block which now occupies the site at Pye Corner is the golden figure of a fat boy. The boy is supposed to personify gluttony, the deadly sin that was said to have brought God's vengeance on the city.

Also in Giltspur Street is the old parish watch-house which was built in the eighteenth century to guard the graveyard against body-snatching racketeers who would steal corpses and sell them on to the doctors at St. Bartholomew'sHospital [9], just across the road.

Under pressure from an expanding city, most of St. Sepulchre's graveyard eventually disappeared but a number of famous people are buried in the church.

One of the best known, especially to Americans, is Captain John Smith [11] , the Elizabethan adventurer who rose to became governor of Virginia.Smith, who worshiped in the church and received communion here before starting out on his many voyages, was a larger-than-life hero who managed to walk unscathed through a string of hair-raising escapades.

Something of the flavour of the man is captured in the poetic eulogy which was engraved on his tomb and is now reproduced on a copper memorial plate near the site of his grave. It begins:

'Here lyes one conquered that hath conquered kings'.

In an age when the ravages of disease and the risks of war often meant a short, if glorious, life, Smith survived to the then ripe old age of 51. He spent his final years in the house next to the church on Snow Hill.

The legend of John Smith is an integral part of American history and the importance of his contribution to the success of the original colonies is beautifully commemorated in a modern window given by his American biographer, Bradford Smith. A statue to John Smith can be found outside the the church of St Mary le Bow [21].

Unfortunately, religious persecution was as much a feature of sixteenth century England as adventure and people of all persuasions suffered for their faith. The first in a long line of Protestant martyrs to go to the stake in the reign of Queen Mary was John Rogers, the vicar of St. Sepulchre's. Rogers had not only published a version of the first Bible in English - a dangerous move, even if the monarch had been a Protestant - he also held controversial views about the nature of the Eucharist. He was executed at Smithfield in 1555 and his remains were brought back to his church for burial.

In more recent times, St. Sepulchre's has built up a close relationship with music and musicians. This stems from its links with Sir Henry Woods, the much-loved founder and conductor of the annual Proms concerts, whose ashes are also interred in the church. Sir Henry (1869-1944) was baptised in Sepulchre's and learned to play the organ here. As a tribute to his life and incredible influence on British music, the former chapel of St. Stephen Harding was rededicated the Musicians' Chapel when Sir Henry died. In a touching memorial, the laurel wreath which is placed around the bust of Sir Henry in the Albert Hall at the start of every Proms season comes back to rest above his tombstone until the next year.

St. Sepulchre's is open on Wednesdays between noon and 3pm or at other times by special arrangement. There is no charge but donations towards the church's upkeep are welcome.

For enquiries, Tel: 0207-248-1660.

Nearest tube: Chancery Lane or St. Paul's (Central Line).

William Penn
&
The Old Bailey

The Central Criminal Court, EC4

William Penn's blind determination to change religious attitudes led to a series of skirmishes with the law and no-one was surprised when he was arrested for the umpteenth time and landed in the dock at the Old Bailey in 1670. What was unexpected, especially in an age when the business of justice was brisk and brutal, was the outcome of the case - an outcome so dramatic that a marble memorial was erected on the spot.

Charged with holding an *'unlawful, seditious and riotous assembly'*, Penn [8] had in fact done nothing more than lead a service of prayer in the street. This had been his response after arriving at the Quaker meeting house he had set up in the city to find it locked against him by soldiers. Hardly an anarchic move by today's standards, Penn's action was then taken as a serious challenge to the established church, which felt itself under threat from a number of non-conformist sects. When he came up for trial together with his friend William Mead, Penn would have expected no mercy.

Within moments of his appearance, though, Penn had staged a logical coup which changed the course of British legal history. Asked if he was guilty as charged, he replied tartly: 'The question is not whether I am guilty but whether the indictment is legal!' He then asserted that a law denying the God-given right of a man to obey his conscience was not valid.

Chaos followed and the furious judge, Sir Samuel Starling, who was also Lord Mayor of London, ordered the jury to return a guilty verdict. But Penn shouted all the louder: 'You are Englishmen. Mind your privilege. Don't give away your right!'

With astonishing courage, the jury actually did pronounce Penn and Mead not guilty. A spectacular battle of wills ensued with the judge first threatening the jurors and then incarcerating them for contempt of court.

The case caused controversy and a review was ordered after the dissidents' supporters produced a writ of *habeas corpus*. In a decision which toppled the old order, Chief Justice Vaughan finally upheld the right of juries to give a verdict according to their convictions.

- The large marble plaque which commemorates the trial of Penn and Mead is preserved in the original entrance lobby of the Central Criminal Court. The building stands on the site of Newgate prison, which was adjacent to the Sessions House where the trial was held.

Visitors should note that, for security reasons, the entrance lobby of the Old Bailey is not open to the public.

The Central Criminal Court, Old Bailey, EC4 is open from 10 a.m. until 4 p.m. Monday to Friday with an adjournment for lunch. Members of the public are usually allowed to watch the courts in session (No bags, cameras and tape recorders. No children under the age of 14.)

Nearest tube: St. Paul's (Central Line)

Benjamin Franklin - A London home

36, Craven St, WC2

Benjamin Franklin's association with London lasted more than 50 years - a period in which the city saw him rise from a penniless journeyman printer to a statesman of international renown. Of several lodgings taken by him during his visits, only one remains - a terraced house which wouod have been quite new when he arrived there in 1757.

Now a quiet backwater just off the Strand near Charing Cross, Craven Street had then been redeveloped as a fashionable area fit for the gentry. Enough of the 18th century buildings survive today to give an impression of its former grandeur, although the facades were altered in the

Regency period.

While the interior of number 36 remains much as Franklin [4] would have known it, from the outside, the house has nothing extraordinary to show. A plaque set into the front wall simply records his five-year residence there without any ceremony or explanation.

In fact, Franklin's mission when he came to England in 1757 formed a crucial part of the sequence of events which led to the American War of Independence. For Franklin, it was something of a Catch 22 situation. At that time, British colonies in the New World were still loyal to the crown so when the French and Indian Wars broke out, the colonies raised taxes to help fund the British defence. Pennsylvania, though, was a Quaker stronghold and many refused to pay the tax on religious grounds. While he had great respect for the Quakers, Franklin suspected that major landholders were simply using this moral stance in order to preserve their profits. When reasonable argument failed, he found himself dispatched to petition King George II for the right to tax these 'proprietary' lands - that is, lands which had been granted to the founder of the colony, William Penn, seventy years before.

The house at Craven Street, then, was home to Franklin while he pressed and won his case on behalf of the Pennsylvania Assembly. His qualities as a statesman were so highly prized, that he was asked to stay on as chief representative of the American colonies.

Franklin returned to Craven Street - although to number 7, which has since been demolished - in 1764, again as the representative of Pennsylvania. Here he was visited by political leaders including William Pitt the elder and the Earl of Chatham. In one of his letters, he recorded how

Chatham called one Sunday morning in 1775 and *'staid with me near two hours, his equipage waiting at the door, and being there while people were at church'.* It was also during this eight-year tour of duty that Franklin was brought before the House of Commons to explain America's objections to the Stamp Act. Although the act was finally repealed, there were soon plans for new taxes on the colonies. He left England in 1775, certain that the result would be war.

- Number 36, Craven Street has been completely refurbished and has now opened as a museum dedicated to Franklin's life and work. As well as exhibitions and artifacts, the house now contains a Student Science Centre and Scholarship Centre.

Benjamin Franklin's house is open Wednesday to Sunday from 10am - 5pm.

Nearest tube: Embankment (District, Circle, Bakerloo & Northern lines) & Charing Cross (Jubilee & Bakerloo).

The Liberty of the Clink

Clink Street, Southwark, SE1

The Clink, a gaol so notorious that its name became slang for imprisonment, stood on the London estate of the Bishops of Winchester which was known as the Liberty of the Clink.

A place of terror for five centuries, the Clink was adjacent to the Bishop's palace, Winchester House, a fragment of which (pictured above) remains on the South bank at Pickford's Wharf.

The Clink was first used to detain anyone breaking the peace within the boundaries of the Liberty. These included prostitutes from the Bishop's own licensed Bankside brothels and their customers. By the 16th century, though, the prison was being used to incarcerate anyone whose religious views countered those of the state. Protestants began to fall into this category as much as Catholics as many started to question and break away from the Anglican tradition. Among the Protestant separatists who were imprisoned as heretics were a group who founded an independent church in Southwark.

Henry Barrowe, John Greenwood and John Penry were Brownists - forerunners of the Puritan movement which led to the emigration of the Pilgrim Fathers [7]. All three were put to death for their beliefs in 1593.

Almost fifty years later, dissenters to a very different regime were confined in the Clink. As bitter disagreements between King Charles I and his Parliament turned to civil war, it became a prison for Royalists. After the war was over, the vast estate of the Bishop of Winchester was sold off and the Clink gaol fell into disuse. Finally, the place housed only debtors.

No more than a dismal hovel, the Clink was burned down in the Gordon Riots of 1780. It was not rebuilt.

Wincester House can be seen from street level.

Nearest tube: London Bridge (Northern line).

Hidden London

Biographies

Contents

John Harvard
1607 - 1638

Born in Southwark, London, John Harvard was the second son of Robert Harvard, a butcher who had moved to the city from Stratford-upon-Avon with his wife, Katherine. Because of the family's connection with both Stratford and Southwark, it is likely that they knew William Shakespeare and his younger brother Edmund.

John Harvard was baptised on 29 November 1607 at St Saviour's Southwark [8], probably within days of his birth. He was brought up in the parish and educated at the church Grammar School where he would have spent long hours studying the classics.

At the age of twenty, Harvard entered Emmanuel College, Cambridge. This choice suggests that he had already decided to join the growing number of Protestants who were moving away from the Church of England to form separatist congregations. The sixteenth and seventeenth centuries were dangerous times for religious dissenters, nevertheless Emmanuel College was known for the puritan ideals of its members and many finally left England for the freedom of the New World.

During his seven years at Cambridge, Harvard met Ann Sadler, the sister of one of his fellow students. When his mother died in 1636 leaving several properties, including the Queen's Head Tavern in Southwark, Harvard had the means to propose to Ann and they were married the same year.

It was around this time, too, that Harvard began to consider emigration. Those whose religious views conflicted with the doctrine laid down by the Church of England were under attack from both King and clergy and by the Spring of 1637, the Harvards were on board a ship to New England. Before sailing, though, Harvard had sold four houses which formed part of his inheritance for £120. The money he made helped to pay for a large collection of books which he took with him.

John Harvard and his wife arrived at their destination in June or July 1637. In August that year, he was received as a townsman of Charlestown (now part of Boston) and in November he was appointed 'teacher' at the church, a post which would have required him to explain the meaning of the scriptures.

Harvard obviously settled well into his new life and quickly won the respect of his fellow colonists. Although he seemed set for an outstanding career, his most significant contribution to his new homeland was to be made on his deathbed. Knowing that the New England colony hoped to set up an educational institution at Newtowne he bequeathed half of his estate and a library of some 300 books for that purpose.

John Harvard died aged 31 on September 14, 1638. As leading colonists decided to rename Newtowne 'Cambridge' in lasting tribute to Cambridge, England where many of them had been educated, they also resolved to dedicate the college being built there to its greatest benefactor. Today, Harvard University is world renowned as a centre of educational excellence.

* There is a stained-glass window in honour of John Harvard at Emmanuel College, Cambridge, England.

Benjamin Franklin
1706-1790

If any name inspires a sense of national pride in Americans it must be that of Benjamin Franklin. For not only was Franklin an outstanding ambassador who fought fearlessly for the rights of colonists in the New World, he was also a great statesman who helped formulate the terms of government following independence.

Scientist, diplomat, philosopher, author, Franklin possessed a rare intellect and an astonishing range of skills. Yet he was a man of simple tastes and self-effacing manner whose natural charm and out-spoken honesty won him respect and affection at every social level.

Born in Boston on January 17, 1706, Franklin was the fifteenth of seventeen children. The family was poor and Franklin had little more than a year's formal schooling before being put into his father's business of candlemaking at the age of ten. He did not take to the work and two years later he was apprenticed to his brother James, a printer. Franklin flourished in this environment and he even taught himself to write news articles so that he could make anonymous contributions to his brother's paper. When this was discovered, the brothers fell out and Franklin had to find work elsewhere.

After an unsuccessful attempt in New York, Franklin made his way to Philadelphia arriving in October 1723. There he quickly made a name for himself but he lacked the experience and financial backing to set up on his own. The provincial governor of Pennsylvania, Sir William Keith, who had by then become a friend told Franklin to sail for London where he could finish his training and buy the equipment he needed to start his own business. He took the advice but the letters of introduction and credit that Keith had promised failed to arrive.

Alone, out of work and with no-one to speak for him, Franklin might have faced a bleak future but with typical determination he soon found himself jobs at two of the leading printing houses in the city. His personal qualities were so obvious and impressive that within two years, he had gained the recognition of a number of important people in literature and publishing.

The ability to win influence at the centres of power was a gift that served Franklin well all his life. While he remained unaffected, he knew how to use it to the benefit of his country when he eventually retired from printing and went into politics. Abroad, he championed the cause of American autonomy, at home, he argued for one nation through united states. In this, as in so many other areas, he had the vision to invent and explore new concepts when others opposed change.

Breaking boundaries was Franklin's passion in everything. Building on the most basic education, he became a distinguished scientist, philosopher and writer. From small beginnings in the print trade, he became an established publisher. As an envoy he commanded the attention of kings and counsellors. As a public servant he won the esteem of statesmen and citizens alike.

An extraordinary man by any standards, Benjamin Franklin nevertheless regarded himself as unexceptional. And although his humility was sincere, he certainly did not lack humour. With a special knack for good sense with a sting, he coined phrases such as: 'Nothing is inevitable but death and taxes' and 'Love your neighbour - yet don't pull down your hedge.'

This blend of perception and wit was characteristic of Franklin and he applied it to everything, including his own mortality. For his epitaph he wrote:

"The Body of B. Franklin, Printer, Like the Cover of an old Book, its Contents torn out, and stript of its Lettering and Gilding, lies here, Food for Worms. But the work shall not be wholly lost: for it will, as he believed, appear once more, in a new and more perfect Edition, corrected & amended by the Author."

The Pilgrim Fathers
1620

The story of the Mayflower and the small band of religious dissidents who boarded her in the hope of finding freedom in the New World must be one of the best-known tales in history.

Determined to win the right to worship according to their own consciences, 101 men, women and children set out from Plymouth, England on a perilous journey across the Atlantic Ocean. Their intended destination was the British colony of Virginia but the Mayflower was blown around 500 miles off course and they finally took shelter in a natural harbour at what later became Provincetown, Massachusetts.

After exploring the area, the travellers disembarked near the head of Cape Cod on December 21, 1620 but arguments had broken out between them over how the colony they intended to found should be governed. This led to the formulation of a binding agreement known as the Mayflower Compact which was effectively the first constitution to be written in America.

Now a unified group, the passengers of the Mayflower established Plymouth Colony, the first permanent settlement in New England. Originally known as the Forefathers, these pioneers were later called Pilgrims, a term which was often used by Puritans and Nonconformists in describing themselves.

William Penn
1644-1718

Freedom of speech and freedom of worship - two fundamental rights expected in modern-day democracies - were privileges which William Penn risked his life for in an age of intolerance.

One of the great forward-thinkers of his time, Penn was hounded for both his ideas and his faith. He held to his principles so firmly that five terms of imprisonment failed to shake his resolve.

Famed today as the founder and first governor of Pennsylvania, Penn arrived in America hoping to establish a community in which liberal-minded people could flourish. Having been the frequent victim of persecution in England, one of his first moves was to draw up a Frame of Government which guaranteed religious freedom for all.

William Penn was born on October 14, 1644 close to the Tower of London, the fortress prison where he was to spend nine months in solitary confinement in later life. Although the exact site of his birthplace is unknown, a letter written in his lifetime places it *'on the east side of Tower Hill, within a court adjoining to London Wall.'* He was baptised at the nearby church of All Hallows, Barking [1].

The son of an important Admiral, Penn was heir to the wealth and influence of nobility. Instead of using his position to his own advantage, he launched into a tireless campaign against injustice. His family connections gave him access to the courts of Charles II, James II, William III and Queen Anne where he argued persuasively for the underdog.

Penn had become a Quaker while studying at Christ Church, Oxford. He was thrown out of university and driven from home by his father because of his beliefs. Undeterred, he travelled Britain, Holland, France, Italy and Germany attracting crowds of two and three thousand with his speaking. Although he was arrested several times, he continued to clash with the authorities and refused to stop even when in jail. To the annoyance of several monarchs, he simply used the time writing books which explained his point of view. The most famous of these, No Cross, No Crown, and Innocency with Her Open Eyes were written in the Tower of London in 1669.

With his erudite arguments and out-spoken ways, Penn was something of an embarrassment to the English establishment. So when he went to Charles II to ask for a grant of land in the New World for himself and his followers in 1681, the King was more than happy to oblige. For one thing, the deal discharged a debt of £16,000 that the crown had owed Penn's father, for another it rid the country of a troublesome sect.

Penn sailed for North America in 1682. In October that year, his ship, the Welcome, reached Delaware Bay where the small settlement of New Castle was already established. Although he owned the land outright because of the king's grant, Penn bought it from the existing occupiers again at its full value. In a typically even-handed gesture, he went on to reimburse the native American tribes for the land as well.

The new colony prospered under Penn's administration but foundered when he was forced to return to England in order to protect its interests at Court. When he went back to Pennsylvania in 1699, Penn found that his deputy had let him down. Having restored peace and order, he sailed for England again in 1701 but he was dogged by political and financial difficulties. Sadly, when he died on July 30, 1718 at Ruscombe in Berkshire, the old crusader was virtually ruined.

John Smith

The hero of Virginia

1580 -1631

Captain John Smith was a swashbuckling adventurer in the finest tradition. Rising from humble beginnings as a cordwainer, Smith eventually went on to become Governor of Virginia and Admiral of New England.

A colourful and heroic figure, Smith won honours in the wars of Hungary in 1602 when he is said to have slain three Turks in single combat and cut off their heads. A grateful Duke of Transylvania awarded him a shield of arms featuring the heads as a result.

Smith was already famous for his escapades in foreign lands when he sailed for the New World from Blackwall in 1606 as part of an expedition sent to colonise the American coast. At that point the group of 144 men was lead by Captain Christopher Newport and it was he who claimed the site upon which they landed for England, naming it Jamestown, after King James I. When Newport returned home, Smith gained control of the new colony and he set about exploring the neighbouring countryside and trading with the natives. As legend has survived to tell, it was on one of these forays that Smith was captured by Powhatan, chief of the local native tribe. He afterwards claimed that he had been rescued from certain death by the chief's daughter, Pocahontas, and he wrote about the adventure in his *Generall*

Historie of Virginia (1624). Whether Pocahontas was responsible for Smith's escape or not, she certainly married one of his group, John Rolfe, who later played a key role in developing the highly lucrative tobacco trade. So prominent was Smith in Virginia's history that his fame earned him a mention two hundred years later in Thackeray's 'Virginians'. He wrote : *"I made acquaintance with brave Captain Smith as a boy, in my grandfather's library at home, where I remember how I would sit at the good man's knees, with my favourite volume on my own, spelling out the exploits of our Virginian hero. I loved to read of Smith's travels, sufferings, captivities, escapes, not only in America, but Europe."*

John Smith returned to England around 1610. He died in 1631 and was buried at the church of St Sepulchre's, Holborn [24], on the south side of the choir. Although the gravestone was damaged and later obscured under a new floor, the epitaph which was engraved on it has been reproduced on a brass memorial plate for the benefit of visitors. Praising Smith's many exploits, the rather saccharine eulogy begins: *"Here lies one conquer'd that hath conquer'd kings!"*